STRONG
WOMEN
BETTER
WORLD

Thank you for joining our team!

With your purchase of *Strong Women. Better World: Title IX's Global Effect*, you are helping the Center for Sport, Peace, and Society provide grants for women and girls who are using the power of sport and education to create a more inclusive world.

All proceeds will be used toward our grant-making program to support women and girls in every corner of the globe.

If you'd like to contribute in other ways,
please follow us on social media and visit our website.

Facebook.com/TheCenterForSportPeaceSociety
Instagram.com/SportAndPeaceUT
Twitter.com/SportAndPeaceUT

Social change is a team sport, and together we can change the world!

ABOUT THE COVER

Strong Women. Better World: Title IX's Global Effect began in February 2020 as a collaborative and ambitious journey to celebrate the strength and resilience of women and their ability to overcome gender inequities. The Center for Sport, Peace, and Society (CSPS) and sisters of the Global Sports Mentoring Program (GSMP) teamed up for what would turn into a much-needed remedial adventure in light of a global pandemic. More than ever, the sisterhood was essential for staying emotionally close while connecting virtually and sharing the beauty of this world together.

Creating this book required trust in our global network to take this bold idea and turn it into a visual representation of female empowerment. We claimed this journey as our mountain and discovered new perspectives on life along the way. This cover exemplifies what can be done when strong women dare to dream, especially while supporting one another.

While the women in this book have made great strides toward conquering the mountain of inequality, we have not yet reached the peak. Strong women in this world have the potential to carve new paths, break gender barriers, and lay the foundations for future generations to inherit a better world.

TABLE OF CONTENTS

FOREWORD

Written by Michelle Marciniak

Hello fellow change-makers.

We're about to embark on a global journey together to meet nine of the world's bravest sportswomen—each fighting for gender equity in and through sports—and each impacted by the work of Dr. Sarah Hillyer and her amazing team at the University of Tennessee Center for Sport, Peace, and Society (CSPS).

I first met Sarah, affectionately known as Dr. Sarah, in 2014 when she asked me to be part of a documentary film she produced titled, Pat Summitt: A Legacy of Love. The film was about a group of young women in Iraq who wanted to play basketball after U.S.-led forces successfully removed the country's authoritarian regime. It was also about my coach, Pat Summitt, and her role in helping Dr. Sarah, and her team, bring the sport to a new generation of girls and women in Iraq.

Knowing first-hand about the power of basketball in a young girl's life, I am honored to play a small part in telling such an important story. Growing up in Allentown, Pennsylvania, all I ever wanted were keys to the local gyms. I wasn't interested in doing anything else other than perfecting my game and growing as a player. The court was my sanctuary, a place where I could recognize my worth and display my authentic self—a self that wasn't like other girls my age.

Basketball was an outlet for building confidence while breaking down gender barriers and social stereotypes. The game gave me an avenue to be the best version of myself. Through basketball, I learned resilience, work ethic, collaboration, pushing beyond limitations, and overcoming adversity. As a Title IX beneficiary, I was fortunate to attend the University of Tennessee on a full-ride scholarship. I obtained my education while being part of two National Championship teams, leading the Lady Vols to our 4th title in 1996.

I wouldn't be who I am today if not for sports and Title IX, the historic piece of federal legislation that, among other things, guarantees girls and women equal opportunity to participate in scholastic sports. Being able to play basketball in college and professionally allowed me to realize my full potential as an athlete. Sports changed my life, and, in turn, I seek to use what I learned as an athlete to make the world a better place. That's what Pat Summitt did for me and countless others throughout her life.

Pat believed in the transformational power of sport and education in a young woman's life and refused to accept anything less than equal access, opportunity, and support. Her role transcends sports as she became an effective and vocal advocate for gender equality. Pat's fight changed the course of my life, and, because of her willingness to push for social change, I reaped many of sports' unique benefits. Succeeding graduation, I competed in the ABL and WNBA, coached at the University of South Carolina, and then became the Co-Founder and Co-CEO of SHEEX, the world's first performance fabric bedding company. I know from personal experience that none of this would have been possible without people like Pat who were willing to dedicate their lives on behalf of women like me, and perhaps like you or someone you know. She pushed the progress of Title IX and changed the lives of girls and women across the state of Tennessee and around the world.

One of the most meaningful lessons Pat taught me was, "The greatest reward in life is a result of sacrificing yourself for another human being to help them become their best." As I've gotten to know Dr. Sarah over the past few years, it's become clear to me that she and her team at the CSPS are no different. By leveraging the unique power of sport and education to empower women working across diverse areas of the sports industry in 67 countries, they are expanding the lessons of Title IX around the world.

While Dr. Sarah has been doing this work for 28 years, it's been the last ten years at UT, where she founded the Center, that she and her team have really scaled their global efforts to protect and promote women's rights in and through sports. I could not be prouder of Dr. Sarah and her team of writers, illustrators, and gender equality advocates.

Strong Women. Better World highlights just how impactful Title IX's long-term legacies are in the global fight for gender equality. Through these inspiring stories, we learn how sports pioneers around the world have benefited directly or indirectly from Title IX, and are helping to move the needle forward in the global fight for equal sports and education opportunities. This book is a testament to the execution of the Center for Sport, Peace, and Society's vision, mission, dedication, and far-reaching impact. There is no doubt in my mind that you will feel inspired to join these modern-day pioneers in the fight for women's rights. Because, while Title IX has accomplished so much, there's still work to do—at home and abroad. The conversation must stay alive.

Enjoy the journey and remember that you, too, have the power to change the world - just like the strong women you will read about here.

INTRODUCTION

Written by Dr. Sarah Hillyer

In July 2007, in Sulaymaniyah, Iraq, camp organizers were eager to start a new basketball training clinic designed to help girls aged 12-18 excel both on the court and in life. This camp wasn't just any basketball camp. It was the inaugural session of the first girls' basketball academy in Iraq since the fall of the country's authoritarian regime nearly four years earlier. The initiative was part of an ongoing effort to build girls' basketball in the region, but the event nearly did not occur as they could only find a handful of flat basketballs. The girls scheduled to participate would be devastated to hear the news.

That's when legendary UT women's basketball coach Pat Summitt stepped in to save the day. Known as much for her belief in the value of sport and education as for her winning record, Summitt emptied out the Lady Vols' supply closet in support of the first generation of girls' basketball players in a post-authoritarian era. "Give them every extra basketball we've got," she said. "Tell those girls that, no matter what obstacles they face, to use this ball to make a difference. Don't ever fear the risks. Go for the opportunity to learn and to become strong young women. We need strong young women. You can be just that and the game can teach you that."

When sixty girls filled the gymnasium on that hot summer morning, they were met with Coach Pat's inspirational words and plenty of high quality basketballs. This snapshot encapsulates the spirit that has driven the work of generations who believe that every girl, every woman, deserves to have equal access to the same opportunities as men, and that individuals can inspire and make a difference.

Strong Women. Better World celebrates the women around the globe who use the power of sport and education to dismantle social, cultural, and political barriers to build stronger, more equitable communities. Within these pages, you'll meet nine members of the GSMP Sisterhood, alumnae of the U.S. Department of State & espnW Global Sports Mentoring Program (GSMP), an award-winning sports diplomacy and mentorship initiative implemented by the University of Tennessee Center for Sport, Peace, and Society (CSPS). Their stories are captivating examples of Title IX's global ripple effect, and they're compelling reasons why American audiences should be all-in to help empower women and girls worldwide to achieve their own Title IX moments.

Title IX, a law enacted by the U.S. Congress on June 23, 1972, states: "No person in the United States shall, on the basis of sex, be excluded from participation in, be denied the benefits of, or be subjected to discrimination under any education program or activity receiving Federal financial assistance." One of the many results of this law is that women and girls have equal opportunities and access to scholastic sports. For fifty years, Title IX has empowered generations, using sport to teach values and skills such as leadership, confidence, resilience, teamwork, fair play, endurance, and strategy. These attributes have benefited women's professional and personal lives, enhancing their abilities to lead, contribute, and excel while enriching societies and strengthening communities. That's why it's important to celebrate this policy and how it has enabled U.S. society to work towards greater gender equality.

Today, most Americans don't think twice about seeing women and girls on the playing field or in the sporting arena. Nor is there much disagreement that female athletes should have the same opportunities to participate as their male counterparts, and that's a remarkable achievement.

Generations of women have broken glass ceilings in the sports world, as well as within U.S. society, through their efforts to create more opportunities for women and girls to play sports. Female athletes, coaches and administrators have inspired countless people of all genders across the United States, who, in turn, have made their own contributions to sports and society. Crucially, and often overlooked, is how these pioneers have influenced women outside of the United States, planting the seeds which today are bearing fruit.

No other country in the world has anything similar to Title IX, yet its impact is felt across continents as U.S. women—the original beneficiaries of Title IX–lead by example through their successes on and off the field of play.

They empower women around the globe to design their own pathways so they don't have to start from scratch as advocates and defenders of equity and equality while enjoying the distinct benefits sport can yield.

Strong Women. Better World salutes these forward-thinking pioneers for making it possible for girls around the globe to achieve their sporting dreams. It also highlights just how impactful Title IX's sports provisions and their long-term legacies are in the global fight for gender equality. It helps provide readers with concrete examples and inspiration for how we can help move the ball forward for equal sports and education opportunities for women and girls, regardless of the country they call home.

STRONG
WOMEN
BETTER
WORLD

"I was carrying all of North Macedonia with me to the top. It is truly amazing to reach a dream of your own life and, in the meantime, make your whole nation proud."

ILINA ARSOVA

Ilina Arsova grew up admiring female heroes on television and aspired to develop her own strength to advocate on behalf of others. The thing that made her happiest was climbing, a hobby she picked up at a young age. At 14, Ilina climbed Vodno Mountain in Skopje all by herself. This first ascent was all it took to captivate her. She invited her sister and schoolmates for group hikes and was determined to climb more mountains, recognizing that she had a natural talent for it. The more challenging and riskier the peaks, the more enticing they became to her. She pushed her limits, leaving the comfort of home for months at a time to scale mountains around the world. For a while, these smaller climbs were enough, but they only amplified Ilina's passion for mountaineering. Wanting to prove that anything is possible, she set out to become the first North Macedonian woman to climb to the top of the world—seven times.

The Seven Summits represent the highest points on each of the seven continents. To undertake this extreme mountaineering challenge, Ilina would have to be in exceptional physical and mental condition. She began to cross-train in other sports such as paragliding, skydiving, bouldering, hiking, biking, skiing, and swimming. However, these were expensive undertakings, and Ilina soon realized that she couldn't afford to train in all of them. She quit paragliding and skydiving and moved towards more specific training needed for the climbs. In 2011, she scaled her first of the Seven Summits, Mount Aconcagua in Argentina. The following year, she journeyed to Africa and scaled Tanzania's Mount Kilimanjaro.

In June of 2012, on Alaska's Mount McKinley, Ilina and her team of mountaineers were attempting to climb Denali, the tallest peak in North America. The trek became more arduous with each passing day. Snow and wind swirled aggressively around them. As other mountaineers were turning around, abandoning the quest, Ilina and her team decided to make camp and wait out the storm. With visibility close to zero, Ilina couldn't see the avalanches, but she could hear them, their ominous rumbles became more powerful, creeping closer to their camp. There was nothing to do but fortify the tents and hope for the best.

The next day, their 14th on the mountain, Ilina managed to exit her tent around 12:30 p.m with temperatures at -40F. Everything had been buried by an avalanche the night before, and several people were injured. Ilina knew that reaching Denali's summit was only the halfway point, and success would not be attained until they descended back down. She was now faced with a life or death decision, not just for

herself, but for her entire team. Ilina could direct them to turn around, go back down to safety, and try again at another time. Alternatively, she could press them forward to complete their mission, putting their lives at risk. As a natural leader, Ilina was built for this. She guided her team back to safety, and Mount McKinley would have to wait for another day.

Then something happened that would change Ilina's life forever.

Ilina was working in Sao Tome, Africa, when she found out that Milena Andonovska, from the U.S. Embassy in Skopje, had nominated her to participate in the inaugural class of the Global Sports Mentoring Program (GSMP). "I remember receiving the official envelope, signed by then U.S. Secretary of State, Hillary Clinton, like it was yesterday," Ilina recalls. "I couldn't believe my eyes, and I knew this was a chance

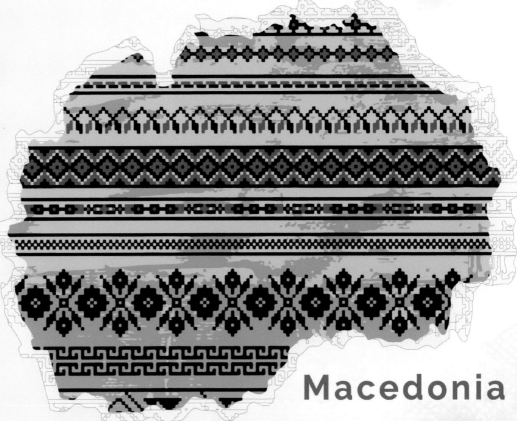

Macedonia

of a lifetime." This was an experience that would no doubt provide brand new opportunities, but it was a decision she couldn't take lightly. Accepting meant she would have to make serious sacrifices—personal, professional, and financial. After careful consideration, Ilina felt that the GSMP had appeared at the right moment, and she couldn't let it pass her by. She quit her job, put her mountaineering dreams on hold, and followed her heart to the United States.

Ilina was matched with Donna Carpenter, co-CEO and co-owner of Burton Snowboards in Vermont. Ilina felt at home in Vermont surrounded by beautiful mountains and snow. Donna's experience in starting a robust women's leadership initiative at Burton was the jumpstart Ilina needed to get her own ideas off the ground. The two women bonded over their shared appreciation of nature, efforts to ensure gender equality, and a desire to increase women's participation in outdoor sports.

During the five-week experience, Ilina was introduced to different aspects of Burton's business, like its Chill Foundation, a nonprofit which provides free outdoor education and snowboarding camps to children from vulnerable populations. Burton's programs seemed to highlight endless possibilities for fundraising and inspiring female leaders of the next generation.

After her invaluable time with Donna, Ilina, and her fellow GSMP participants, traveled to

Washington, D.C. They attended workshops, visited community-based organizations, and developed action plans to create sporting opportunities for disadvantaged populations back in their countries. When the time came to return to North Macedonia, Ilina made the trip home with an abundance of enthusiasm and a renewed commitment to fight for justice on behalf of all women and girls. She also carried with her the strength and support of her GSMP sisters and her mentor, Donna.

Ilina got to work as soon as she arrived home. Drawing from her love of mountaineering, her action plan was to create a center for outdoor education. She built a space, IKAR Hut, to share her stories of climbing and encourage girls to turn their own dreams into reality. IKAR Hut is situated in a neighborhood near beautiful Lake Ohrid in North Macedonia, a UNESCO World Heritage Site, and is surrounded by stunning mountain views.

The program offers cultural tours of Ohrid, a variety of outdoor adventures aimed at teaching life skills and fostering a love for nature, and art workshops, as art is Ilina's second passion. The building itself is made of eco-friendly materials, and old objects are never trashed, but are turned into beautiful pieces of art. Implementing her action plan was only the beginning. After experiencing the unique power of women working together to achieve a common purpose during the GSMP, Ilina wanted to pay it forward. With determination, she pushed legal entities, such as federations and national sport agencies, to accept the idea of promoting gender balance in sports.

Though working at IKAR Hut brought Ilina great joy, she still had five summits to scale. Refocusing on this goal, Ilina successfully ascended Mount Everest, the highest point on Earth, in 2013. After accomplishing this milestone, Ilina was overcome with emotion. "The last steps up towards the top of the world were really exciting," she remembers. "There is a moment when you know

you have the summit even before you are actually there, and it can be really emotional. That is when my frozen tears got stuck between my cheeks and the oxygen mask. That is when my bag felt super heavy, as if I was carrying all of North Macedonia with me to the top. Mountaineering sports had never received a big response or public reaction before this. The whole country was cheering for me. It is truly amazing to reach a dream of your own life and, in the meantime, make your whole nation proud."

Even though the whole country was celebrating her achievement, returning home after Mount Everest was not easy. Ilina felt like the richest person in the world on the inside, but she was a national hero struggling to make ends meet. Her sponsors' financial support hadn't been enough, so she had sold almost everything of value she owned, including her paintings and her car, to fund her expedition. She had lost her job, and her gender activism had yet to gain the momentum she'd hoped it would. Ilina still needed to pay back

the loans she took out to complete Mount Everest, and, with four peaks yet to ascend, she could no longer afford to climb.

Then Donna Carpenter called. Ilina's GSMP mentor asked her how things were going, and Ilina talked about her situation, happy to connect with her friend and mentor. The very next day, Ilina was shocked to receive a Western Union money transfer from Donna. "I will never forget that," she says. Thanks to Donna's contribution, Ilina was able to continue her quest for the Seven Summits and also focus her love and energy on her GSMP action plan, IKAR Hut. In a short time, things were returning to normal for Ilina, the word spread about IKAR Hut, and seeds were planted for other organizations representing women in sports.

Ilina traveled to Russia and scaled Mount Elbrus in 2014, but the shadow of Mount McKinley still loomed over her. Ilina had made the wise decision to suspend the climb when the weather became too unstable to continue safely on her first attempt in 2012. She later learned that four climbers had lost their lives that fateful day, so the decision to discontinue the climb had proven life-saving. Ilina and her team may have turned around that day, but she never intended to give up. "Somehow I knew that McKinley would give me another chance," she says. That chance came in 2016, and it resulted in a successful summit. Ilina was the first North Macedonian female on the roof of the North American continent.

After the successful Mount McKinley climb, Ilina conquered both Puncak Jaya in Indonesia and Mount Vinson in Antarctica in 2019, becoming the first North Macedonian woman to scale each of the Seven Summits and one of only around 70 women worldwide. In response to her accomplishments, North Macedonia now recognizes mountain sports for female athletes for the first time in its history. Ilina has twice been nominated for the "8th of September" award, her country's highest government sports award, and received the prestigious "11 October" award from the city of Skopje, as well as other accolades from municipalities, cities, and the Mountain Federation.

As Ilina's reputation continued to grow, so did her realization of the power of social and digital media as effective cultural and social influencers. Inspired and encouraged by her mentor Donna, whose words "This is herstory not history" rang in Ilina's head for years, she began a video production company and directed a documentary series titled HerStory. This was a second iteration of her original GSMP action plan, in which she documented the stories of female athletes living in countries where gender inequality, particularly in sports, is commonplace. This vast undertaking required much time and a great deal of financial resources. Fortunately, Donna and Dr. Sarah Hillyer of the Center for Sport, Peace, and Society (CSPS) were there to help. Both Burton and the CSPS became partners on the project, and in January of 2019 Ilina released the first set of short films featuring Balkan female athletes. These films garnered three awards for mountain films and earned official selections at many prestigious international mountain film festivals.

In addition to being an award-winning documentary producer and world-renowned mountaineer, Ilina is also an accomplished artist. She graduated from the Faculty of Fine Arts in Skopje in 2005 and had her first solo exhibition, titled "Landscape without Censorship," a year later. Ilina's passion for mountains is clearly displayed in her art. She draws inspiration from the societies, people, and cultures she experiences throughout the countries she visits for her climbs. She uses art to address some of the problems she sees in the world—problems in ecology, consumerism, and gender equity. Mountain scenery often takes center stage in her art, as Ilina admires its powerful, steep lines breaking the horizon.

Ilina is considered one of the finest athletes her country has ever known. The reputation and credibility she has built from climbing the Seven Summits will aid her as she prepares to complete more projects and confront old and new challenges in the fields of rock climbing, alpinism, and high-altitude mountaineering. While she prepares for her own next steps, Ilina continues to hold events for girls, sharing her experiences accumulated over the years. She admits to them that it is not easy to wake up early and train every day, but the reward is always worth the effort. Ilina explains that in sport she found the best way to overcome difficult situations, recognizing that the way she approaches climbing helps her solve problems in life. "Every step counts," she says. "The decisions you make are crucial and there is no time for regrets. If you get stuck, don't blame others, just train harder and try again."

The massive mountains of gender inequity may seem impassable, but Ilina Arsova knows what it takes to scale mountains such as these. She's done it seven times.

DONNA CARPENTER'S TITLE IX EXPERIENCE

Donna Carpenter grew up with a love for sport through skiing and horseback riding. She also developed a passion for fencing, eventually landing a coveted spot on the Columbia University varsity fencing team. "I was always the fourth person on varsity, so I had to work my tail off to keep that spot," she recalled.

At the time, in the early 1980s, women only competed in the foil fencing events, not saber or epée. "We never questioned it," she said, but the next generation did. The first U.S. Olympic fencing gold medal since 1904 was won by Mariel Zagunis for women's saber in 2004.

Growing up, Donna had a general awareness of Title IX's sports provisions, and of its ability to change women's experiences and participation in sports. In fencing, Donna recalled that she and her teammates were taken seriously, and that the resources were fairly equal to their male counterparts. "We had no [female] role models," she noted, "but we really were given the same travel budgets."

Donna gained and improved a variety of skills thanks to playing sports, including how to work as part of a team, fighting for what you want, discipline, and preparation, as key ingredients to success. She also learned the difficult lesson that women were held to different standards. "In order to compete," she said, "you have to be that much better, that much more prepared, take it that much more seriously. Women had to be better."

"It's so critical that Americans care about the Title IX experience, legacies, and worldwide impact," Donna emphasized. "Of course, it makes sense that you would have equal resources because of what sports provide, that sense of discipline, that sense of leading a team, leadership, focus, and purpose."

Donna knows that not everyone sees the importance of sports. Some argue that providing equal access for women and girls to play drains resources from men's sports. They see women's sports as less significant, citing that they are not heavily consumed or commercialized, nor do they drive revenue at the same level as men's sports. "They don't see it as a win-win," she said. "It's a zero-sum game to those who think that way."

That's why it's crucial to remind people of Title IX's import and impact, to ensure that we don't take it for granted, and to help others globally benefit from the lessons and advances incurred. "It is talking more about the resistance and exposing that resistance, calling it out for what it is: sexism."

"Sport changes the way we see ourselves. It gives value, it gives purpose, and it gives you the chance to see how hard work pays off. The vast majority of female CEOs played sports. It's more than just access to sports. It's ultimately access to resources and power."

"Be strong. Believe in yourself. Fight for what you want. If you feel something strongly in your heart, you can get through the bad days. If you're doing what you love, there will always be more good days than bad."

CARLA **BUSTAMANTE**

At the young age of 12, Carla Bustamante had applied for, and was awarded, the opportunity to be a junior reporter for the local newspaper covering the 1997 Caribbean Series baseball tournament. She made it to the field and stood next to the only female news reporter, surrounded by the players from Mexico, the Dominican Republic, Venezuela, and Puerto Rico. All Carla had with her was a list of questions her dad helped her write and a small voice recorder. She was supposed to interview a player of her choice, but Carla was awestruck, having watched these players on television with her family. Out of place and unsure that she could muster the courage to talk to any of them, she stood motionless. Then, seemingly out of nowhere, she felt a hand on her shoulder and heard the reporter say, "Don't be scared. He's going to answer your questions." That little push was all Carla needed.

By the time the day was over, Carla had interviewed the famous Francisco "Paquín" Estrada, the manager of Mexico's team, covered two international baseball games, and had shoes covered with dirt from the baseball field. Upon returning home, she told her mom that she didn't want to clean her shoes. Instead, she would see the dust and remember this incredible day forever. Though her mom eventually made her dust off the shoes, nothing could scrub the events of that special day from Carla's mind. The shy girl from Hermosillo felt brave and her dream of one day becoming a sports journalist was born.

Growing up, Carla's family enjoyed watching baseball together. She remembers nights huddled around the television, watching whichever team was playing. Her brother, 12 years her senior, worked for PepsiCo's marketing division, requiring him to visit ballparks where Pepsi was a sponsor. Occasionally, he took his little sister with him and talked to her about the game, which only amplified Carla's growing interest. When her father told her about the ad in the local newspaper inviting kids to apply to be a journalist for a day and cover the Caribbean Series, Carla didn't hesitate to apply.

Now the experience was etched in her mind: the energy and clacking typewriters of the newsroom, abuzz with reporters from around the Americas writing up their stories. What Carla didn't see in that newsroom—or later in her mind's eye as she revisited it again—was other women. She and the female reporter who had encouraged her were the only two, and it turned out that the woman didn't report on sports. She was usually assigned to cover big, cultural events. Carla wondered why there were no women in the media room. Was she dreaming to think that she might someday work in a room like this? Or would she be expected to get married, have children, and focus solely on domestic duties?

After graduating from the Universidad de Sonora with a degree in communications, Carla experienced several uphill battles as a young female pursuing a career in sports journalism. "When I started at Telemax as a 16-year old intern," she recalls, "my coworkers were

confused. They would ask, 'Why would a woman want to work in sports?' They asked me if I was sure, even offered me an internship in the news, entertainment, or production areas, but I wanted to be part of the sports journalism team." Despite the pushback, Carla persisted and finally convinced them to give her a chance. She was grateful for the opportunity to pursue her dream covering sports on the field, even if she was the only woman.

In 2006, the Naranjeros de Hermosillo, a professional baseball team, hired Carla, who was only 20 years old, as a Public Relations director. This was a very important position in the Naranjeros organization, and Carla took her trailblazing role very seriously. However, those she encountered weren't so welcoming, and Carla was treated as though she was trying to break into an exclusive boys' club. They couldn't believe that a television station would send a woman to report on a baseball game, on the field no less. Whispers began to circulate.

"A girl is here. What is she doing here?"

"She must be a player's girlfriend."

"Maybe she's with one of the higher-ups at the television station or baseball club."

"That bothered me . . . a lot," Carla says. "They always wanted to 'involve me' with someone else, to say that was the only reason I was there." Not one of them was willing to look past her gender and evaluate her on merit, her interviewing skills, or her passion for the game. The rumors escalated to the point where she was ready to quit, but

Carla's parents didn't raise a quitter.

Even as the noise grew around her, Carla continued working to improve her journalism and marketing skills. She spoke with her boss about the rumors, and he reassured her that the reason she was there is because she was well-versed in the game and well-prepared for the job. "Show them the real reason you are here," he advised her. With the support of her boss and her friends, she began working on her confidence and self-esteem and learned how to manage the gossip. "I chose baseball, and, in many ways, baseball chose me," she says. "It is something I really love. This gives me the strength to continue. Working as an on-field reporter for those four years was my favorite job." She loved the work so much, she says, she would have done it for free.

True to her commitment to always take the next step to improve, Carla began working toward a master's degree in 2009. In 2011, she graduated with a Master of Science in Marketing and International Trade. This degree helped Carla sharpen her skills and broaden her vision for the business of baseball, not just the game as a sport. Carla used her position as a Public Relations director to improve many things in the Naranjeros organization, implementing several new strategies with the team.

Then, in 2015, Carla was stunned to receive a call from the consulate informing her that she had been chosen to participate in the Global Sports Mentoring Program (GSMP). She traveled to Bristol, Connecticut, where she was partnered with Marina Escobar, Vice President for Visual Technology at ESPN. The match was thrilling for both of them. "Marina is a strong Latina who understands Latin American culture and issues," says Carla. "She knows exactly where I am coming from." Marina also felt an immediate connection. "From the moment we met," Marina says, "Carla felt like a daughter, a friend for life."

During her time with Marina at ESPN, Carla honed her interpersonal and time management skills and took a deep dive into creating growth opportunities for women through sports. he also watched Marina closely, amazed at her power, confidence, honesty, and ability to balance work and family. For Carla, Marina was a model of strength and a pillar of support. "I learned how to be strong," she says. "I came to understand that Marina will be there for me forever and always." By the end of the program, Carla found herself part of a sisterhood fielding similar obstacles in their own countries, a member of a league of extraordinary women who lifted each other up through it all. This life-altering experience bolstered her confidence and pushed her to pursue new goals. "I arrived in the United States with many fears," she says, "and I still have fears, but the way I think about them has changed." Carla was ready to return to Mexico to implement her vision.

Softball was alive and well in Hermosillo, and the skill level of the players was outstanding, but there were no opportunities for girls to play baseball. Carla began by organizing a baseball clinic just for girls, the Mujeres en el Diamante (Women in the Diamond), in partnership with the U.S. Consulate in Hermosillo. She wanted to open the doors of baseball for girls in Mexico, so she invited Justine Siegal, the first woman to coach for a Major League Baseball (MLB) organization in the United States, to lead the clinic. Two hundred and fifty girls had a chance to learn baseball from an inspiring woman who broke many glass ceilings in a male-dominated sport. Siegal commended them on their high level of play and encouraged them to apply for scholarships and keep playing. Watching girls play baseball at the Naranjeros de Hermosillo stadium, during a clinic Carla organized, was like something out of *A League of Their Own*. This was a place where the Hermosillo Naranjeros (men and boys) had always played, and Carla had hopes that one day the Naranjeras (women and girls) would play there, too.

There was even more in store for Carla in 2015 than she knew at the time. Throughout her career, she had been inspired by Jessica Mendoza, a decorated softball player who served as the first female booth broadcaster for the NCAA's College Baseball and Softball World Series in the United States, commentator of an MLB game, and senior advisor to an MLB team. Carla saw a little of her own life story in Jessica's, and she was impressed by Jessica's ability to overcome the obstacles in her own way. When Carla saw that Jessica was going to be at a conference in Phoenix, Arizona, talking about MLB's spring training, she knew she had to get there somehow. She was certain that she could learn from Jessica—about baseball, clinics, journalism, life—and Phoenix was as close to Hermosillo as Jessica might ever get, which was still ten hours by bus.

Carla had never traveled on a public bus by herself, so she was scared, but she couldn't let this window of opportunity close. Her GSMP sister from Indonesia, Hanna gave her the push she needed. Carla says, "She said I would be okay and should try it, so I bought the bus ticket. The departure time was 12 am, and Hanna was text messaging me the whole time. She was asking me how I was and repeated to me every time she texted that I was going to be okay." She drew strength from her GSMP experiences and sisters and was determined to

meet Jessica Mendoza face-to-face. Then, she would work to convince Jessica to come to Hermosillo to help with another baseball clinic for women and girls.

When the bus arrived at the hotel, Carla didn't have a reservation, so she didn't have a room. She had been traveling on a bus for ten hours and wanted to change her clothes, brush her teeth and freshen up, so she visited the restroom in the hotel lobby. The conference would take place in this very hotel the next day. When Carla walked out of the restroom and back into the lobby, Jessica Mendoza appeared in front of her. "Oh my god!" Carla blurted, awestruck to be standing in front of one of her heroes. "Jessica Mendoza!"

"I was surprised to see Jessica so quickly. I was there wondering how to enter the conference, and there she was!" Carla went to her, introduced herself, and told Jessica her story—how she wanted to meet her at the espnW Summit in 2015 but couldn't, about the GSMP, her career, coming by bus to Phoenix just to see her—all of it. Needless to say, Carla has no regrets for taking a trip to find and meet her hero. It's just another reminder in Carla's life that if you want to achieve something special, you cannot let fear stand in your way.

Today, the little girl who didn't want to clean the Naranjeros de Hermosillo field's dirt from her shoes is the head of communications for the very same team. She still has the newspaper that printed her first article when she was only 12 years old, and even had an opportunity to reinterview Francisco "Paquín" Estrada, now a team manager, who says, "I was happy to be her first interview." Carla now organizes that same event she attended as a kid. Carla loves watching the kids live the experience that shaped her whole life when she was their age. She encourages others, especially young girls, to follow their dreams. "It won't be an easy path," she tells them, "but it's already a little easier than it was before. Be strong. Believe in yourself. Fight for what you want. If you feel something strongly in your heart, you can get through the bad days. If you're doing what you love, there will always be more good days than bad."

In a 2019 interview with Fronteras Desk News, Carla said, "I think it's very important to have a role model, to be able to see that something is possible and say, 'I want to be that, too.'" Carla is now that person for so many little girls and young women in Mexico. She has stepped up to the plate again and again, recruited heavy hitters, and now, thanks to her vision, the bases are loaded for Mexico's girls.

MARINA ESCOBAR'S TITLE IX EXPERIENCE

Marina Escobar grew up during the 1960s and 1970s ensconced in the realm of soccer. Her Colombian family watched the sport on television, but at an early age she found herself wondering, "Where are the girls' teams?" She wouldn't be able to watch women's soccer matches on TV until the first women's World Cup in 1991. "Amazing to think that it took that long," she said.

Yet soccer wasn't her sport of choice as an athlete. Marina ran track and field during high school but wasn't very conscious of gender inequities in sports at the time. She did notice, however, that her track meets and competitions never received the same exposure or attendance as the boys' events did. Her team also didn't garner the same attention. "I enjoyed track and field, and was a good sprinter," she noted of her successful on-track efforts, "but I felt that I was not coached to do my best, nor did I aspire to push myself. If I had a female role model, would I have strived more?" It was far different back then compared to today.

Being an athlete shaped the person Marina is today. The traits first honed on the track, such as accountability, selflessness, resilience, leadership, and communication still serve her today. So do lessons in teamwork. "I learned and practiced the importance of diversity on a team which undoubtedly lends itself to success," she said.

Marina knows it's important to realize that it isn't just individual girls who benefit from Title IX's sports and education provisions. It's a multiplier effect. "My children have benefited from these life lessons [gained from my sports career]," she noted. "Boys, too, learn the importance of good sportsmanship and how to deal with different personality types." The lessons learned from sports help everyone. "Why would a parent not want their child to have the right to those benefits?"

"GSMP has already had a ripple effect.
Having women like Carla go back to their
countries with an action plan to advance
gender equality and equities through
sports is a stepping stone, a ripple to a
larger wave."

Title IX "prohibits discrimination on the basis of sex in education programs and activities operated by recipients of Federal financial assistance." This landmark U.S. legislation's sports implications have since enabled women and girls to benefit in myriad ways from equal opportunities to play sports as part of their scholastic experience—a unique regulation found nowhere else in the world.

The 2020 Tokyo Olympics showcased Title IX's longer-term legacies, just one of the many examples in recent years. The XXXII Olympiad was the first in which nearly 49% of athletes were female, and more than half of the 613 Olympians who competed for Team USA were women. American female athletes won 66 of the United States' 113 medals, including 23 of the country's 39 gold medals, out-earning their male teammates for the third straight Summer Games in a row. Moreover, if Team USA's female competitors constituted their own country, their medal count would still have been higher than that of any other country except for China and the Russian Olympic Committee.

Inarguably, the majority of these Olympic heroes were able to train and pursue their sport at its highest levels through U.S. university and collegiate sports programs. According to the NCAA, there were approximately 650 current and former NCAA women's sports athletes who competed at the Tokyo Games.

The U.S. national soccer and basketball teams are among the most mediatized of all women's sports, and most visibly illustrate the long-term benefits and legacies of Title IX.

In the eight FIFA women's World Cups since 1991, the United States has won four titles, one vice-championship, and three bronze medals, while the team's Olympic accolades include four gold (1996, 2004, 2008, 2012), one silver (2000), and one bronze (2020) podium finish.

Not only is the soccer team one of the sport's most dominant of all time, its successes have helped shine the spotlight on women's sports more broadly. Since the United States hosted—and won—the 1999 FIFA World Cup, the national team has moved into the mainstream, and front pages, of sports media, eclipsing their male counterparts and putting women's soccer into everyday lexicon and popular culture references. They've also significantly boosted the numbers of girls who now play the sport, inspired by the '99 team, which has resulted in new generations of female players who have continued to infuse the national team with some of the world's best talent. Whether celebrating on-pitch successes, using the power of labor to obtain better working conditions, suing the U.S. Soccer Federation for equal pay, or speaking up against social injustices and sexual harassment, the team and its generations of players continuously personify the strength of character fostered through playing sports.

It's on the basketball side that the impact of Title IX is most stark. In 18 FIBA World Cups since 1953, the United States has amassed 10 championships, one vice-championship, and two bronze medals. The American women dominated early FIBA global competition, snagging first place at the inaugural 1953 tournament in Chile and at the 1957 edition in Brazil. Although, they failed to reach the podium in subsequent World Cups, losing to the East Europeans and East Asians, until 1979. That was the year Team USA, which Pat Summitt coached after years as a player, once again won the world championship.

Despite the 1972 enactment of Title IX, the NCAA did not recognize women's basketball as a sport until 1980, thus little funding or attention was paid to women's sports. That began to change in the late 1970s after women's basketball debuted at the Olympic Games in 1976, and the NCAA wrested control of women's collegiate sports from the Association for Intercollegiate Athletics for Women (AIAW), placing additional pressure on funding college basketball programs.

The United States repeated as FIBA World Cup champions in 1979 and has placed in the top three in every World Cup since then. Within Olympic competition, the United States clinched second-place in 1976, with Summitt still playing, but were denied the opportunity to go for gold in 1980 due to the U.S.-led boycott of the Moscow Games. Four years later, they earned their first Olympic gold medal at the Los Angeles Games and have medaled at every subsequent Olympiad, including a record-setting seven consecutive gold medals since 1996.

Soccer and basketball may be among Title IX's most visible beneficiaries, but they are far from the only ones.

"Previously, I thought I could help Taiwan win more gold medals. Now, my priority is to make Taiwan a better country."

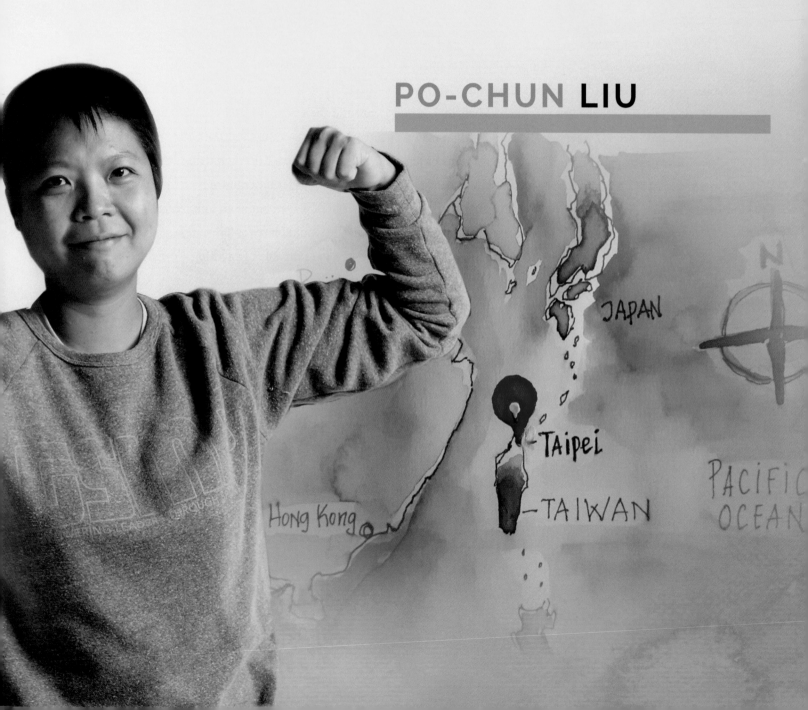

PO-CHUN LIU

JAPAN

N

Taipei

TAIWAN

PACIFIC
OCEAN

Hong Kong

Po-Chun Liu's loving parents supported her every endeavor. Before she could even walk, Po-Chun's father would take her to the baseball diamond to teach her about the sport that would come to shape her life. As a child, she watched game after game, her passion for baseball growing unchecked. Po-Chun desperately wanted to play this game that had so captivated her, but at this time in Taiwan there were no girls playing baseball. Still, her father's support never wavered. He would say, "You are capable of anything, Po-Chun." Buoyed by his encouragement and her faith in herself, Po-Chun grew up believing that she would make baseball history.

Po-Chun experienced gender discrimination first-hand at age 13 when she went to tryouts for her junior high school's baseball team. She had been playing recreational baseball for years and was determined to impress the coaches and players with her skills and prowess. Her enthusiasm was soon smothered, however, when they refused her the chance to show them what she could do. "No skirts allowed," they said. "Girls play softball." Po-Chun knew then what injustice felt like, but she felt too young to speak up. At that moment, she felt powerless.

Po-Chun refused to let those junior high coaches extinguish her love for the game. Baseball had helped her grow strong, confident, and disciplined, and she refused to give up on her dream. She decided to volunteer with Little League Baseball, where she assisted with summer camps and began interpreting for the Taiwan Baseball

Association during international competitions.

Though she loved volunteering with Little League, Po-Chun suspected that this work would not further her aspirations to make baseball history, so she kept a vigilant eye out for anything that might do so. One such opportunity was to serve as an interpreter for the Taiwan Baseball Federation, which allowed her to travel to tournaments around the world. As Po-Chun watched her beloved game, she was stunned by the poor quality of the umpiring. "I could do a better job than this," she thought. She began to wonder if her journey to make baseball history wasn't as a player, but as an umpire, and if this was the trail she would blaze for Taiwanese women.

"You are capable of anything, Po-Chun," rang her father's voice in her ears. Once again, Po-Chun drew from her inner strength and determination and pushed forward, taking her first steps on the journey toward becoming a certified umpire.

In 2006, she completed her umpire training and was ready to take the field. Her very presence was offensive to the men around her. Players told her that they didn't want women on the field, and she was thrown out of dugouts. Fellow umpires warned her not to touch any of the equipment, claiming it was bad luck and would result in errors and injuries for the players. In rooms of 20 to 30 umpires at tournaments, she was ostracized, sometimes humiliated. It would have been easy for Po-Chun to throw in the towel, but she refused to give up on her dream just because some men didn't want her there. Instead, she focused even more on her craft and became the best umpire she could possibly be.

After a few years serving as a base umpire, she was ready to start calling balls and strikes. Once again, though, it seemed that everyone was conspiring against her—there wasn't even proper home plate umpire gear for a woman.

At one multi-day clinic for an umpire license, she was told every day to give up. Po-Chun calmly produced the receipt that confirmed her payment for the clinic. "I will keep showing up," she vowed.

Finally, in 2009, Po-Chun's perseverance was rewarded. That year, the New York Yankees came to Taiwan to play, and Po-Chun was assigned as their interpreter. When the Yankees heard her story, they offered to sponsor her and pay for the gear necessary to umpire behind home plate. Suddenly, she had everything she needed to become the first-ever female international baseball umpire from Taiwan.

There was no reason for Po-Chun not to umpire a game—she had the training, the experience, the passion, and now, the gear—but Taiwanese baseball was still not ready to see a female umpire. She was kicked off the field again and again, even when she volunteered her services for free. Frustrated, she shared her misfortunes with a confidant who urged Po-Chun to go abroad to get opportunities to practice. It was in Hong Kong, while umpiring

a women's baseball tournament, that Po-Chun caught the eye of Marc Gooding, a well-known international umpire. During the week-long tournament, he mentored her and then invited her to umpire an international tournament in Australia. Po-Chun used her personal savings to book the flights.

In 2010, she made her World Cup debut as an umpire at the Women's Baseball World Cup in Maracay, Venezuela. It was this experience that solidified Po-Chun's belief in the empowering possibilities of baseball. She realized, however, that not everyone would be able to use their savings to book flights to travel for these opportunities. That's when it hit her—if Taiwanese girls didn't have the means to travel abroad, she would bring the wide world of baseball to them.

She began making plans to host an invitational tournament consisting of four women's teams from Taiwan and a women's team from Australia. Po-Chun would use her own money to book the Intercontinental Stadium, the best ballpark in Taiwan. Again, she encountered resistance. The number of people, women included, who thought that girls didn't deserve to play in this stadium shocked Po-Chun. Still, she pressed on. The invitational tournament would be held at the Intercontinental Stadium.

Women playing in this space was a momentous occasion, and Po-Chun wanted to make it memorable. As the players entered the stadium, Po-Chun had each of their names displayed on the giant scoreboard. Even now, ten years later, she still receives messages of gratitude from those who participated. The experience made them feel worthy of baseball, worthy of that stadium, and empowered to play. For Po-Chun, this first initiative to empower women and girls only strengthened her commitment to organize baseball clinics for girls and women in Taiwan.

When the American Institute of Taiwan (AIT) introduced Po-Chun to the Global Sports Mentoring Program (GSMP) in 2017, she knew at once that she wanted to participate. Having never had a female mentor in Taiwan, she was thrilled by the thought of finally having someone to consult with on her journey. Once chosen, she was paired with National Hockey League (NHL) Senior Vice President Susan Cohig in New York, who knows a thing or two about breaking the ice in a male-dominated sport.

Susan works diligently to support women's hockey at every level and enhance visibility for the women's game. She helped Po-Chun sharpen her marketing, sports management, networking, social media, and fundraising skills.

"Susan is very wise and kind," says Po-Chun. "She taught me not only how to make my plan work, but also how to be a better person. I am so lucky to have such a great mentor. Her impact will last a lifetime." This life-changing experience empowered Po-Chun, encouraged her work, and gave her a mission, not just for herself, but for all of society. It also helped her refine her vision. Though her baseball clinics were successful and beneficial for the participants, she realized that even more could be done. "My original wish was for them to have fun, to put a smile on their faces," Po-Chun says. "The GSMP helped me realize that this was actually empowerment and that I could build further upon it." After a conversation with NHL Commis-

sioner Gary Bettman, Po-Chun had another important epiphany—that sports are designed to help you become a better person. "Previously, I thought I could help Taiwan win more gold medals," she says. "Now, my priority is to make Taiwan a better country."

Given the opportunity to reflect on the mission of her baseball clinics and her own past, Po-Chun was finally able to put words and feelings to her own experiences as a 13-year-old girl. "People think that because laws are providing equal rights, there

is no gender discrimination anymore in Taiwan. Laws are one step, but the second step is the implementation and, most importantly, the real-life experience. Every girl can realize her full potential and take charge of her life, if given a fair chance." Having internalized that empowered women can only make a country better, Po-Chun left the United States and her GSMP family knowing that she was not alone and that her sisters echoed her father's sentiment: "You are capable of anything, Po-Chun."

Upon returning to Taipei, Po-

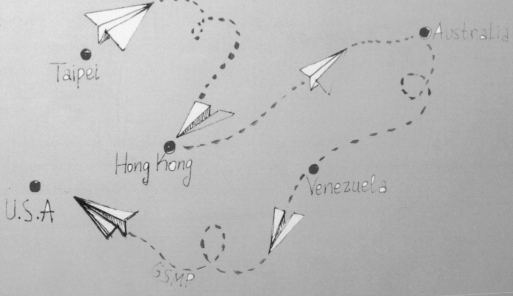

Chun laid the groundwork for a sports center where she could host various programs, including a GSMP-inspired mentoring program for women. With the support of the broader GSMP alumnae network in Taiwan and the region, she co-organized 17 women's baseball games and a number of girls' training camps, benefitting more than 14,000 participants.

In addition to her umpiring duties, Po-Chun works as a project manager and full-time social worker for The Garden of Hope Foundation, an organization that serves female victims of domestic violence, sexual assault, and sex trafficking. Working closely with girls and women who didn't believe they were worthy of good things opened Po-Chun's eyes even further to the needs of women across Taiwan and strengthened her resolve to provide access to empowering experiences for them.

Po-Chun appeared on the Forbes 2018 List of Most Powerful Women in International Sports. The following year, on the sidelines of the Commission on the Status of Women (CSW) at the United Nations headquarters in New York, she was awarded the International Olympic Committee (IOC) Women and Sport World Trophy. Never one to rest on her laurels, she then began a Ph.D. program in religious studies at National Chengchi University and is using sport and education as platforms for dialogue among people of various religions. Currently, she is using baseball to demonstrate a different perspective on gender equality in Muslim countries. "Allowing women and girls to picture and discuss their futures," she says, "is bringing hope to everyone."

On March 8, 2020, at the dawn of a worldwide pandemic, Po-Chun launched Sport for All, a non-profit organization that will allow generations of women and girls to benefit from the power of sport and education and ensure a legacy that will continue long after she retires. Also in 2020, she collaborated with Yu-Hsien "Blue" Tseng, a 2013 GSMP alumna and Associate Professor at National Taiwan University, to found the Women's Sports Association Taiwan. This effort offers a platform and a safe space for women and girls in sport, with a long-term vision of having scholars develop materials to improve gender equality in sport and design experiences for teachers. Last but not least, Blue and Po-Chun are supporting the start-up magazine *Women—Discovering Asia's Women in Sports*.

Believing that she has a responsibility to make the world better, Po-Chun has made a lifelong commitment to serving the underprivileged through sport. She feels deeply that sport can change lives across all backgrounds, wants to see greater financial support for women's sport, and has spoken to Parliament to advocate for greater female representation in government. "I want to help Taiwanese girls believe that they have the potential to take charge in their lives despite traditional stereotypes," she says. "I know sports can make a difference, because that is what happened to me." Po-Chun shines bright on the

field while helping others to do the same. That's what leaders do—they fight to open doors and keep them open for others. Although she has already accomplished so much, she remains focused on empowering girls and women to pursue their own happiness.

Now known as the "Mother of Women's Baseball," Po-Chun has achieved her dream of making baseball history. It took grit and perseverance to become who she was meant to be, and she dared to do something no woman had done before.

SUSAN COHIG'S TITLE IX EXPERIENCE

Susan Cohig grew up swimming competitively, winning four consecutive state championships with her high school team. Although Title IX was passed just before she began middle school, the legislation's sports provisions were not part of her active consciousness at the time, despite her family supporting equal rights and participating in rallies.

For Susan, being a competitive swimmer had numerous benefits. "[It taught] independence, self-reliance, resilience, and other things that served me in taking risks when I went to college at the University of Denver," she said. She also found a community. "I was part of a team, despite swimming being a very individual sport," she recalled.

It wasn't until the FIFA 1999 World Cup, held in the United States, that the implications of Title IX really pierced her consciousness. "It was incredible for me to see the whole country get behind these amazing female athletes and their accomplishments," she recalled of that summer's victorious U.S. Women's National Team. "Even though I was working in sports at that point, I honestly didn't see the embrace of women as athletes." That got her thinking about the many ways that being a swimmer helped to create the person she is today.

For Susan, it's important to call attention to Title IX's sports benefits, to make people more cognizant of the many ways it feeds into the sports ecosystem—as well as society at large. "You have to emphasize what sports does for young men and women, girls and boys, how it's making them stronger people who are better able to contribute to society," she said. "We know it's important that girls and boys have the same opportunities, we recognize the value of it—not because they're all going to be professional athletes. If we believe in the benefits of all the things that the United States' ideals stand for, then everyone having equal access to sports is part of that."

"As a country, we are so invested in what sport can do for boys and not what it can do for girls. When the U.S. won the World Cup in 1999, I started understanding, primarily through the lens of soccer, how many girls were inspired to start playing and what that experience did for them in terms of developing confidence, team building, and other skills used outside of sports."

Did you Know?

Pat (Head) Summitt was one of Title IX's biggest champions, but her life is far more than a mere sports story. It's one that began with changing the world of women's basketball in the United States and ended up changing the world.

Summit was born in Clarksville, Tennessee, and grew up working on her family's dairy and tobacco farm, which she credited for generating her work ethic and drive. She graduated from Cheatham County High School in 1970 then attended the University of Tennessee-Martin where she was an All-American athlete, leading her team to a 64-29 record during her four-year career. In 1974, she earned a bachelor's degree in physical education, and that same year, at the age of 22, Summitt was hired as the head coach of the University of Tennessee's Lady Vols. During her first two seasons she did it all: coached the team, drove her players to games, and washed their uniforms—all while earning a master's degree in physical education and training for the 1976 Montreal Olympic Games.

Summitt coached the Lady Vols from 1974 until 2012 and compiled 1,098 wins, 8 NCAA championships, and 32 combined Southeastern Conference tournament and regular-season championships. She ended her nearly four-decade career with a winning percentage of .840 and was the first NCAA basketball coach to reach 1,000 career wins. In her 38 years at the helm, Summitt coached 21 All-Americans, 14 Olympic Team members, and 34 WNBA players.

She is credited with bringing women's basketball to center stage, thanks to her keen understanding of how to achieve representation and positive attention through all forms of media. Summitt made it impossible for sportswriters and sportscasters to ignore her team by providing all of the key reporting components—player information, statistics, and game notes—needed to craft coverage. Moreover, she had amazing athletes, which helped her to boldly create the demand.

Pat Summitt was not just a basketball coach, she was a teacher of life lessons who empowered young women to believe in themselves. The hardcourt was where Coach Summitt, who was equal parts intense and empathetic, taught valued principles. Her players learned that it was ok to be strong, fierce, intense, competitive, and demanding, but also to treat people with kindness, humility, and thoughtfulness.

One of her most striking statistics was the 100 percent graduation rate for all of her players who completed their eligibility. Coach Summitt demanded excellence and inspired her young athletes to be the best versions of themselves on and off the court. Lady Vols were known for sitting in the first three rows of the classroom and were forbidden a single unexcused absence, a demonstration of respect that Coach Summitt instilled into each of her players.

An iconic figure, Summitt helped lay the foundation for the growth of women's sports through her accomplishments and promotion of equal rights for women and girls. She earned her reputation as a pioneer whose success eclipsed the basketball arena and encouraged women to reach new heights. She was not just a championship coach; she fostered a championship spirit in every person she met.

In 2012, Summitt stepped down from coaching after being diagnosed with early-onset dementia, Alzheimer's type. True to her unwavering strength of character, Coach refused to sit idly by. She created a foundation to raise money for Alzheimer's research and worked to raise awareness of the disease.

"I thought I would be remembered for winning basketball games," she said, "but I hope I'm remembered for making a difference in this disease."

Summitt passed away in 2016 at the age of 64. She was the true embodiment of leadership, integrity, and strength, and through her illustrious career helped change the trajectory of women's sports in America and across the globe. Perhaps her most enduring influence is found in the relationships she cultivated along the way.

"I won 1,098 games and 8 national championships," she stated, "but what I see are not the numbers, I see their faces."

"I want to inspire girls to
contribute toward creating
a strong female force in
Bangladesh."

ASHREEN **MRIDHA**

Ashreen Mridha was introduced to basketball by her father, who was in charge of sports management at the school she attended. As a small third-grader, she remembers holding his hand and sitting on the ground for hours as they watched the senior women's team practice, keenly studying the strategies and techniques of the game. Ashreen remembers, "I used to observe what they did and try to do those things myself." She wanted to play basketball, too.

Unfortunately, Bangladesh in the early 1990s still operated under a traditional patriarchal system of gender norms, and most fathers weren't attentive or supportive of their daughters playing sports. Fortunately for her, Ashreen's father was an anomaly of sorts, and supported her passion and love for basketball. "Many of my friends were jealous," she remembers. "They would often ask me 'Hey, why don't you get your dad to talk to my parents?'"

With the support of her family, Ashreen joined the Basketball Federation Training School as soon as she was old enough. In Bangladesh, there was a common belief that girls shouldn't—or couldn't—play basketball; Ashreen saw it as rejection without a valid cause, so she set out to prove them wrong. "Every time people around me—friends, family, coaches, federation officials—made me feel like I

wasn't allowed or didn't deserve the same opportunities as my male counterparts, it filled my heart with anger and distress." She practiced harder, pushed herself more intensely, and took every step necessary to accomplish her dream. Ashreen's time in the gym paid off, as she was selected to be part of her school's basketball team. Unfortunately, once she moved up to high school, there was no basketball program, so Ashreen had to search for one. She found a local team, The Wildcats, and polished her skills while playing club ball.

Upon graduation, Ashreen enrolled at North South University in 2009, hoping to continue her basketball journey alongside her education. To her dismay, she found that the university didn't have any women's sports

teams. "I felt out of place and lost to be studying somewhere with no opportunities for women to play sports," she says. "There were some days when I didn't feel like going to classes, like all my previous basketball training and preparation was a waste." She often grumbled to her father that she wished they could afford for her to study abroad so she could continue playing basketball in a place where it was socially acceptable. Ashreen and her friends complained together about the lack of women's sports teams, questioning why there were no opportunities for women when men had cricket, football, basketball, and every other kind of sport available to them. They wondered if there was a shortage of interest, or if no one was willing to invest in a women's basketball program on campus.

Ashreen was willing. It was time for her to take ownership and the actions necessary to create something from nothing. She was told that campus administration was not welcoming of the idea of developing a women's sports team because they didn't deem it "socially acceptable." Undeterred, Ashreen discussed the idea of organizing a women's basketball team with her friend Nabila, and Nabila was all in. "We sat together in the university computer lab," she remembers, "and we designed a poster on Microsoft Word. We printed 100 copies and pasted them all over campus. There was not a single doubt in my mind that we wouldn't find 12 girls interested in basketball."

The posters became a topic of discussion among students. "We heard many boys talking about these posters around campus," she recalls. "They were laughing at the idea of forming a women's basketball team, as if girls playing sports was a joke. I was determined to break that mindset." She persisted, tuning out the pessimism, mockery, and discouragement. "I knew that I only had to do this once, because if a team came into place, it would be there for as long as the university exists." Her dedication paid off, and Ashreen formed the first-ever North South University women's basketball team.

Her persistence paid off. Ashreen formed the first-ever North South University women's basketball team.

That same year, she was recruited to Bangladesh's women's national team, one of 12 women selected from a field of over 50. Again, Ashreen's father's support proved invaluable. Practices were held twice a day—early morning and late evening—and she lived about an hour away. It wasn't safe for a teenage girl to take public transportation on her own. Her father, the only one in the family who could drive, woke up every day and drove her to practice between 5 and 6 a.m., went to work, and then drove back to pick her up after the evening practice. "He never complained," Ashreen explains. "He even took the first picture of the national team and printed three copies. The first one he framed and gave to the federation, because they had no pictures of girls playing any sport hanging on the walls of their offices. He gave the second one to the team captain, and he gave the last one to me."

She still has it hanging on her wall.

Ashreen was proud of her time spent on the national team, but she knew work still remained, as traditional gender roles continued to dominate society. "These roles dictated that a woman's place was in the home, behind the man," Ashreen says. "It certainly was not on the basketball court." It was during her time on the national team, however, that she met Ibrahim Mohammad, a member of the men's team. Ibrahim shared her passion for the sport and, even more importantly, supported her hoop dreams, something Ashreen had never thought she would find in a partner. They married in 2017, and Ibrahim became Ashreen's best teammate and biggest cheerleader.

Ashreen was eager to share the positive aspects of basketball with others, so, in 2018, she founded Deshi Ballers, a nonprofit organization that hosts women's basketball training camps and tournaments, giving young women more opportunities to compete than Ashreen was ever afforded. "I don't want the next generation of girls in Bangladesh to go through the same struggle," she boldly states. "I want every girl to dream and wake up able to turn that dream into reality." Deshi Ballers provides a safe and supportive space for girls to not only improve their basketball skills, but also equips them with the necessary tools to reach their full potential off the court.

When she filed the paperwork to form Deshi Ballers, she had to declare who the chairperson would be. "Of course you'll be the chair," Ibrahim said without hesita-

tion. "I'm just here to work for you." Here was yet another man in Ashreen's life who, like her father, stood next to her as she used basketball to raise awareness of the need for gender equality.

Ashreen knew she was fortunate to have the support from her father and husband. The same could not be said for all Bangladeshi women, who generally lacked the autonomy to make decisions and live their passions. "It comes from years and years of interpreting religion in the wrong way," Ashreen believes. "It's ingrained in our culture where women are made to feel like they're here as caregivers or servants, and sports are something only for recreational purposes. Women are expected to either play at the highest level or give it up and raise children. In my opinion, you shouldn't have to play only professionally to justify your passion."

Being surrounded by men who championed her success, didn't mean Ashreen had an absence of obstacles. Support from media outlets and the basketball federation was virtually nonexistent, relegating women's basketball to the shadows. Ashreen began to feel this burden. "The only reason you have pursued this for so long," many told her, "is because you made it to the national and professional level. Otherwise, you wouldn't have been able to fight this battle." Even though she was involved in numerous activities for the development of women's basketball in Bangladesh, there was no substantive national framework in place. With little financial and emotional back-

ing, Ashreen felt like she was working alone.

Furthermore, gender inequities were not exclusive to basketball, and female athletes in other sports were fighting to have a voice in that same battle. Ashreen is determined to be that voice. "For me, it's more than basketball," she says. "I want to be an advocate for women who play all sports. The kind of injustices that I have faced just in my small community, I can't imagine what so many women in other sports have faced." Changing a culture, however, isn't an easy task; there are consequences for speaking up. Ashreen knows of one male cricket player who aired his grievances about the lack of resources for his team and was banned from competition for two years. It's hard to imagine the result of a woman doing the same, but Ashreen refuses to be silent. She says she is "happy to go through that for the sake of girls who come after me, because, at some point, there's going to be progress. At some point, there's going to be change. I look forward to seeing more girls standing up for themselves. So maybe ten or twenty years from now, girls won't have to fight this fight. I want these girls to take the skills and values learned at Deshi Ballers into other spheres of life and become strong, successful humans. I want to inspire girls to contribute toward creating a strong female force in Bangladesh."

In 2018, hoping to expand upon the success of Deshi Ballers, Ashreen applied and was selected to participate in the Global Sports Mentoring Program (GSMP). She was mentored by Laura Dixon, then Head of External Relations for Spurs Sports and Entertainment in San Antonio, Texas. This pairing was a dream come true for Ashreen, as Laura was the first female sports mentor she had ever had. Laura wanted to know what Ashreen hoped to learn from the program. She really listened to fully understand her goals and vowed to help make them happen. Laura vowed to help make them

happen. She organized meetings with people she knew would inspire Ashreen and give her ideas of how to develop and implement her projects.

Under Laura's guidance, and with the help of others in the Spurs organization, Ashreen learned how to effectively fundraise for nonprofits, grow an audience on social media, and increase engagement of female coaches in her community. Laura coordinated several opportunities for Ashreen to tell her story and communicate her action plan to large audiences, both in-person and through podcasts. The impact of this was invaluable to Ashreen, particularly the speaking engagements. "While I was repeatedly sharing my story on different platforms," she remembers, "my purpose became clear. I was ready to give interviews and presentations more confidently."

While in San Antonio, Ashreen watched her first in-person NBA game—the first in the Bangladesh female basketball community to do so. She remembers that after watch-

ing Becky Hammon, the first female assistant coach in the NBA, run practice, she went back to her hotel room and cried. "It was an emotional time for me," she recalls. "In Bangladesh, a men's team would never take a woman seriously." Ashreen was deeply impressed with the way Hammon approached her job, admiring her organizational skills and preparedness for both practice and games. She was in awe as she observed Hammon take the lead during timeouts. "And Coach Pop [Gregg Popovich] was letting her!" Ashreen exclaims. "She knows the game and her role very well. Players under her realize that she knows what she's doing, and they respect her for it. They don't see her as a woman; she's just a coach."

Perhaps the most impactful part of the GSMP was that, for the first time, Ashreen saw her work with women's basketball in Bangladesh celebrated. Not only did her GSMP sisters recognize her work, but they also supported it. Ashreen no longer felt alone, because she had a global family that would always be there for her.

Ashreen strives each day to make Deshi Ballers even better, channeling her inner Becky Hammon. She describes Deshi Ballers as a community of girls who play and train together." When a tournament comes up, players have to earn their position on the team by showing up every day to practice and compete. "I never have a fixed set of girls in my mind," Ashreen admits. In doing this, she hopes to create strong mindsets among the girls of Deshi Ballers, for she has firsthand knowledge of how basketball skills translate to life. "Never stop," Ashreen implores her players. "Never let anything get in your way. Be fearless. No matter what, keep going. Take that Deshi Baller spirit and mindset forward. We can't leave any of it behind. Keep pushing for progress. One day we'll have our own Title IX.

One of Ashreen's coaches once asked her, "Are you willing to spend the next 25 years of your life with women's basketball?" For Ashreen, there was only one answer. She has already empowered women throughout Bangladesh, but she's not finished. She has plans to be the country's first female basketball coach, to develop a professional league as big as the WNBA, and to construct a state-of-the-art indoor basketball arena for women. "It only takes one," she says. "If there are one or two people who think like me and who share this vision, then the effect will go on."

LAURA DIXON'S TITLE IX EXPERIENCE

Laura Dixon grew up in Texas playing sports, but Title IX's significance didn't stand out until she was a young professional working in the sports industry. As a twenty-five-year old at a Women's Sports Foundation conference, she had the opportunity to play tennis with Billie Jean King. "She was very gracious and made time to spend with us," Laura recalled. That encounter with an original Title IX pioneer left a deep impression.

Throughout her career, Laura reaped the benefits that come from playing sports. In addition to skills like leadership, teamwork, and the ability to communicate, she said, "one of the lessons I've learned is I've never been afraid of hard work." It's an important aspect, because women, more often than not, have to work harder than men in their positions. "It's a shot in the arm that we still have so much work to do, that we do better when we do it together, and that there's a lot of opportunity for more advancement," Laura said. "We'll get there faster when we go together."

Development for such a transformative policy takes immense effort. "I didn't really appreciate that until I was in the GSMP world," she explained. As part of the program, she learned more about women's equality and access to sports and education — or lack thereof — in other countries and was able to contrast those realities with what

Title IX has helped provide. It was an eye-opener, as was her own start in the policy-making world. "Seeing the amount of energy and effort that went into passing a bill at the local level made me marvel at how much time and talent went into getting Title IX policy passed, especially 50 years ago."

The Name, Image, Likeness ruling has brought Title IX once again to the forefront. The decision, passed in June 2021, enables NCAA student-athletes to be financially compensated by a university using their name, image, or likeness in a school's marketing and advertising campaigns. "The ruling opens up new business opportunities for athletes and athletic departments, for the private sector, the public sector, for whomever wants to play in that space," Laura said. "There's a huge upside for female athletes, but the downside is that it has the potential for athletic departments to focus on sports where they're able to compete from a Name, Image, Likeness standpoint." That's why she's thankful Title IX is in place, for it helps to protect sports, especially women's sports, from being cut.

"A Title IX Institute, where women and men from all over the world could research and collaborate to develop policies and understand how they could be implemented within their home structures or systems, would be pretty powerful."

"Success is not about the things you have but rather the value you create in sharing with others."

CYNTHIA COREDO

Born in Nairobi, Kenya, Cynthia Coredo was the third of four children. She and her siblings were often expected to help their parents with household chores and to run errands for their mother, who was pregnant with a fifth child. On a seemingly ordinary morning, Cynthia and her older sister, Quinter, were tasked to pick up items from the local market. Cynthia was young, only ten years old, and Quinter wasn't much older. They knew the route to the market; it was a trip they had made countless times, and it wasn't a far walk. Side by side, they made the trek, repeating their grocery list aloud to not forget what their mother needed, "Milk and bread." As they made their way to the market, Cynthia and Quinter noticed a crowd surrounding a man lying still in the street. Suddenly, the man's face came into view. It was their father.

After the death of her husband, Cynthia's mom struggled to make ends meet for her five children. In 1997, much like today, life in the poverty-stricken areas of Nairobi was difficult, and their mom had no recourse but to send Cynthia and Quinter to live with their grandmother in a small, countryside village. A normal day included using candles as the main lighting source, going to the mountains to gather firewood and to the river to fetch water, and farming with their grandmother to grow food. Then, when Cynthia was only 13, she learned that her mother had died. Living through all this with tremendous determination, she recalls the good in her life, remembering her surroundings as beautiful and green.

Cynthia's grandmother was something of a visionary, though, and did everything she could to offer her granddaughters a chance to live better lives. One decision was incredibly impactful; her grandmother found places for her granddaughters in an orphan's school operated by Catholic nuns from Ireland. Unable to afford tuition, Cynthia would bring firewood for the volunteers to cook the girls' porridge each day in exchange for her education.

Going to school was a long hike, around six miles round trip through the bushes. The opportunity to go to school, however, was a blessing and a privilege, and Cynthia was quick to realize it was worth the effort. She knew that education could amplify the strength that grew within her and give her access to things beyond her current reach. Having already faced more adversity than the average 13-year-old, Cynthia was building the grit, resilience, and perseverance that would propel her toward a successful future.

Cynthia became a star pupil and earned a scholarship to secondary school. She was grateful for those who believed and invested in her, and she vowed to let nothing shake her confidence or determination to empower others. As she swept the floors of the school one day—a way for her to say thank you to the nuns who gave her the opportunity to study—she made a promise to herself. "You are going to be a woman for global change, helping others find their path just like you are given a chance now." She was inspired by the actions of an elderly woman

known as "Granny" who lived near the school. Granny gifted part of her land so that the school could be built and girls could gain access to education. As an expression of her gratitude, Cynthia often checked in on Granny to care for her and deliver necessary groceries and supplies.

Cynthia knew the value of giving back. "Faith played a strong role in my story and helped me to stay hopeful," she says. This faith guided her when she lost her parents. In those dark times, Cynthia always remained true to her vision and strong—not only for herself, but for those around her. "Cynthia has to love Cynthia," was a daily mantra and reminder of the power of self-confidence and compassion.

Just when things seemed to be looking up for Cynthia, life landed another blow. Her older sister, who was looking after their younger siblings, died of tuberculosis in 2006. No one was able or willing to take in orphans, so, at age 18, Cynthia gained custody of her younger brother and sister. Just as her grandmother had done for her, Cynthia prioritized education for her siblings, working various jobs to make sure their school fees were paid.

Driven by her determination to empower others, Cynthia began working as a volunteer tutor for Box-Girls Kenya in 2007. This organization uses boxing as

an entry point to tackle the cultural issues affecting girls and women. Cynthia was drawn to boxing as an athletic activity because of its connection to her own life. It is a sport that demands both physical and mental strength, control, and dedication. Matches take place in a limited space where you must use your knowledge to face your fears. It's not just about punching; it's also about taking a punch and getting back up. Cynthia could relate.

She continued to pour her energy, time, wisdom, and skills into BoxGirls and rose through the ranks until she was named program manager just a year later. In this new role, Cynthia coordinated sport and leadership programs aimed at making girls stronger, more confident, and goal-oriented. She saw herself in the eyes and lives of the under-privileged girls participating in the program, and always encouraged them to believe that anything is possible. "I've been through everything that you have," she expressed to them, "from sanitation issues to violence. You can choose to give up, or you can work on yourself, your talent, and try to keep your hopes up." She wanted them to know that there would always be someone in their corner, in and out of the ring.

As Cynthia's responsibilities grew, so did her achievements. In 2013, she was a facilitator for the United Nations Office on Sport and Development for Peace (UNOSDP) Youth Leadership Program in Gwangju, South Korea. The following year, she spoke at the United Nations Educational, Scientific, and Cultural Organization (UNESCO) World Youth Forum on Sport, Culture, and Peace in Nanjing, China. Cynthia was well on her way to becoming a global agent of positive social change.

Then, in 2015, she was awarded the opportunity to meet like-minded women from around the world, and her support system multiplied.

Cynthia was selected to participate in the 2015 class of the Global Sports Mentoring Program (GSMP). Even though she felt a bit overwhelmed about representing her entire country, she looked forward to the opportunity to renew her vision for BoxGirls and beyond. She was paired with mentor John Lisko, Executive Communication Director, co-mentor Emi FitzGerald, and their team at Saatchi & Saatchi in Los Angeles, California. John and Emi empowered her with the tools, ideas, and resources needed to develop her own entrepreneurial model. Equipped with new strategies and renewed determination, Cynthia returned to Kenya feeling stronger than ever. She knew that the support of her fellow GSMP participants—a global network of women she had come to call sisters—Cynthia would become who she was always meant to be.

Working with BoxGirls Kenya, Cynthia developed opportunities for girls and women to gain access to boxing and to discuss the issues facing their communities. Yet, Cynthia wanted to do even more, so she created Footsteps, a foundation which could provide the three-punch combo that girls in Kenya needed. At Footsteps, Cynthia

builds on the power of sport to help uphold the character and ethics of girls benefiting from the program, but sport isn't the only focus. The organization also offers training in job and entrepreneurial skills, both of which Cynthia feels she gained from her grandmother. She vividly remembers how her grandmother would bake sweets and have Cynthia sell them to the school community during breaks so they could buy soap and food. Through her work at Footsteps, Cynthia is living her passion, that of transformative leadership and mentoring. She is laying a foundation for Kenya's girls to be empowered, to design their own lives, and to cultivate a new energy and mindset.

Building on the strengths she has developed, Cynthia is now creating a civic movement that advocates for the rights of girls and women. Her dream is to use sports as a platform for self-discovery, leadership development, and to afford every girl a fighting chance. Cynthia believes in the power of sport to unite communities while encouraging self-confidence in each individual athlete. Cynthia's journey has taught her to trust her inner voice, to invest in herself, and to connect with those who support her. The message she wants to instill in girls and women is that life is going to knock you down at some point, but when it does, "use your gloves wisely to fight back and give a hand."

Two years later, Cynthia—along with her GSMP sisters Geraldine Bernardo (Philippines), Dima Alardah

(Jordan), and Dr. Sarah Hillyer—was preparing to step onto the stage in front of a huge crowd to accept the Stuart Scott ENSPIRE Award on behalf of the GSMP. This award is given yearly, in honor of the late ESPN sportscaster Stuart Scott, and celebrates those who have courageously used sports as a tool to create a more peaceful and equitable world.

As Cynthia stood backstage, she could see the presenter, Laila Ali—the former professional boxer who compiled a 24-0 record. She was awestruck. It was an amazing moment for Cynthia to receive this award from one of the most decorated boxers in the world, and she knew that this was a dream come true for many at BoxGirls Kenya. Cynthia thought back to her young self sweeping the grounds at school, and how she had vowed to become a woman for global change. Now here she was, being acknowledged on the international stage having done just that. After a short video highlighting their respective programs, Cynthia heard, "Please welcome from Jordan, Dima Alardah, from the Philippines, Geraldine Bernardo, and from Kenya, Cynthia Coredo."

Cynthia walked onto the stage and faced the cheering crowd. This was, without a doubt, an emotional and life-defining moment—it was proof that she was an accomplished global activist. She used the platform to celebrate others and her community, wearing a necklace representing the journey of life that had been handmade by a Kenyan artist.

The girl from the slums of Nairobi ended up landing the uppercut by having all sorts of experiences thrown at her, building grit, resilience, and perseverance. Life has been a tough opponent for Cynthia at times, but she welcomed the hard hits, learned from them, and punched back. Losing her parents and sister were blows that could have knocked Cynthia out, but she has proven that with hard work and a vision, you can create something beautiful in life. She knows that success is not about the things you have but rather the value you create in sharing with others. Through Footsteps, Cynthia is sharing her knowledge, power, and vision with Kenyan girls in need of a helping hand.

JOHN LISKO'S TITLE IX EXPERIENCE

Title IX was passed at a time when the United States tried to level the playing field and provide opportunities without barriers of discrimination. "Title IX was truly a foundational game changer," John Lisko said of its ability to empower generations of women and girls to benefit from the educational aspects of playing sports.

However, it wasn't until he became involved with the Global Sports Mentoring Program (GSMP) that John began to more directly understand Title IX's longer-term implications on reshaping the U.S. workforce. "I really see a difference for how colleagues perform in an organization," he said of how former athletes collaborate and help build a strong working environment that empowers all to thrive.

The GSMP experience underscored to John just how unique the 1972 U.S. legislation remains. "I learned in Year One of the GSMP [2012] about how in the United States, sport and education go hand-in-hand and give a person individual strength and determination," he observed. "That's not the case elsewhere in the world, where it's either sport or education."

That's why, for John, it's important to educate people, especially younger generations, about Title IX and its trailblazers who have left such rich legacies for subse-

quent successors. "Too many people today take Title IX's sports provisions for granted," he said.

According to John, it's imperative for all Americans to better understand how Title IX has benefited society as a whole, including the corporate workplace. In addition, the landmark legislation provided momentum that can translate to other countries, similar to how GSMP alumnae are utilizing the tools gained through their sports mentorship experience to break down social barriers back home.

"To me, that's the core of what the GSMP is. The power of sport is that it brings people together. We can use such moments to bring people together around the world to make it a better place."

EMI FITZGERALD'S TITLE IX EXPERIENCE

Emi FitzGerald grew up in Texas playing sports, notably basketball, track and field, and cross country. She was captain of her school's varsity track and cross country teams and won a Texas 4A state title in the 800m run. Although she opted not to compete during college, she always understood that Title IX afforded her the opportunity to make that choice. "I am certain that I would not have had the opportunities to compete had Title IX not existed," she reflected.

She credits the 1972 legislation for forcing schools of all levels and sizes to do better in providing girls equal opportunity to participate in sports. "I could not be a bigger advocate of Title IX because it changes mindsets," she noted of how the mix of sport and education and its emphasis on equality translates into professional workforces.

Emi pointed out how her on-court experience helped her to develop traits that serve her well in the business world. From leadership skills, confidence, and processing and overcoming failure, she acknowledges how much she was shaped by being an athlete. "That is such a core component of who I am today and my working style," she noted.

For Emi, the benefits of sports and education have greater impacts on the world. Having more equal processes and procedures in place can help transform societies, and measures as seemingly simple as providing females equal access to sports can make a difference. That's why she's an advocate for a global Title IX. "We can't know how far we can go without knowing how far we've come, and then seeing the opportunities Title IX confers from a global scale," she said. "In the United States, we've taken for granted what Title IX has done, but for women, and especially women in underprivileged situations, it can help put them on more equal footing."

"It would be incredible if the United Nations had a resolution to institute and enforce Title IX on a global level, so that societies worldwide can realize the wide-ranging ripple effects of sports and education."

The Center for Sport, Peace, and Society (CSPS) at the University of Tennessee-Knoxville was launched in 2012, but its foundations are built upon the decades of activity and endeavors of its founder, Dr. Sarah J. Hillyer. A direct beneficiary of Title IX's sports provisions, Hillyer credits the legislation with the numerous ways that the gift of sport and education opened the world to her. "Both became a round-trip ticket to the world for me and I became their dedicated ambassador," she said of the opportunities sport and education provided.

Hillyer worked in the Sport for Development and Peace (SDP) sector long before it was named as such or recognized by the United Nations (UN) in 2000. In 1994, she founded the nonprofit organization, Sport 4 Peace, which facilitated sport-based projects aimed to promote peace, solidarity, and mutual understanding. It placed an emphasis on gender, disability rights, and the psycho-social well-being of displaced persons due to war, violence, and/or natural disasters.

Recognizing the need to do more than the scope of her remit, Hillyer turned to the University of Tennessee's Socio-Cultural Studies department. She was accepted into their doctoral program, and focused on rigorous research, to demonstrate proof of concept for the use of sport to advance gender equality and promote peace between nations, and competitive grant writing, to better advocate for significant financial investments to empower women through sport, education, and social innovation.

As a graduate student, Hillyer began to work with Pat Summitt at her annual summer basketball camps. Their special working relationship was fueled by their passion for sport and the life lessons it can impart to women and girls. Thus, when Hillyer was set to travel to Iraq in 2007 and was in dire need of basketballs, she called upon Summitt. The two collaborated again in 2009 to bring 15 participants of that inaugural basketball camp to Knoxville to meet Coach Summitt and thank her for turning their dreams into reality.

Hillyer continued her international work at the intersection of sport, education, and gender equality. Between 2009 and 2011, she and the U.S. Department of State's Sports Diplomacy Division (then SportsUnited office) continued, albeit sporadically, to work together on various projects. Hillyer led workshops for their programs on topics such as sport and peacebuilding, conflict resolution, and women's empowerment for various Sports Visitor delegations coming through Washington, D.C. The on-again-off-again collaboration, coupled with the 2009 Iraqi basketball partnership, provided Hillyer with critical insights into U.S. sports diplomacy, a rapidly evolving field.

In 2012, Hillyer launched the CSPS to expand the footprint of solidarity through sport-based social change. Just four days after its inception, the Center was named the sole implementing partner of the U.S. Department of State's Global Sports Mentoring Program (GSMP)—an initiative that aims to empower women and girls through sports. Along with the work through her foundation, Coach Summitt supported the Center's mission and was appointed by then-Secretary of State Hillary Clinton to the GSMP's Council to Empower Women and Girls through Sports.

The CSPS honors Pat Summitt's legacy by working to help global leaders develop innovative solutions to sociopolitical challenges through sport, working to create a more peaceful, equitable and inclusive world. At its founding, the CSPS was considered "a new and innovative outreach, engagement, and research endeavor" at UT. Hillyer's focus rapidly moved from its international work as a non-profit organization to working globally through higher education to administer the GSMP, enabling its successful maturation into one of the U.S. Department of State's flagship exchange programs.

"Every time I stand up to fight it's a win-win because I'm learning so much and helping to forge a path for others to follow."

ALINE **SILVA**

BRAZIL

South America

Atlantic Ocean

In 2006, no one believed that Aline Silva could medal at the Junior National Wrestling Championship. Brazil was just establishing itself in the sport, and Aline didn't have the same level of experience as her competitors.

Aline had spent countless hours training for this moment, but, as she looked at the other athletes, she realized that they had been preparing, too. Each of them was a strong competitor. Each of them was going to wrestle to the best of her abilities. Each of them believed in herself. Still, Aline had a feeling. As she looked out at the other wrestlers, she thought about all she had endured, and everything her mom had sacrificed. "I deserve to be here," she told herself. "I deserve this win."

***

Aline was raised by a single mother, and life wasn't easy for either of them. They were a family familiar with struggle, and it seemed like the odds were always stacked against them. Through the hardship, Aline learned to overcome challenges at every turn.

One of those challenges was coming home from school each day to an empty house. Aline's mom worked long hours to support them, sometimes juggling two or three jobs just to make ends meet. Because her mom had to work, Aline often found herself unsupervised and started skipping school. At 11, she looked much older and, just wanting to belong, began hanging out with a group of kids who were smoking and drinking. Things went from bad to worse, as Aline's excessive drinking habits caused

throughout the ordeal seared itself into her psyche. "I've never forgotten the shame that fell on my mother," she says. "She was reproached by everyone for not taking care of me when she did everything humanly possible to simply house and feed me." Not only did people criticize her mom, they judged Aline as well, assuming she was already a lost cause. This lit a fire inside her, and she vowed to turn her life around.

More changes came in short order, as Aline's mother began to make decisions about where Aline could find a fresh start. She wanted Aline to have better access to after-school programs that would provide the safety, structure, and supervision she needed. One such decision was to transfer her to a school that happened to have a judo team. Aline found herself captivated by the movements—she loved the sport's grace, strength and strategy—and decided to try it. Little did she know how fortuitous this decision would be.

Aline fell in love with judo. It made her feel powerful and in control of her own body and mind. She wanted to become a great athlete—the best, in fact—and she knew she was going to have to fully commit herself to get there. She understood that she had been given a second chance at life, and she wasn't going to waste it.

Judo taught Aline responsibility, discipline, and focus, and her coach immediately saw the potential that Aline was also beginning to see in herself. He inspired her to make necessary changes, and he became an important,

countless sleepless nights and considerable anxiety for her mom. The situation came to a head one day when Aline drank too much and fell into an alcoholic coma. She was on the verge of death when her neighbors found her lying face down in the middle of the street.

Fortunately, Aline made a full recovery, but she would never be the same. The way the doctors treated her mom

positive presence in her life. Aline's coach treated her like one of his own. "He invited me to take part in club training outside of school," she remembers. "He gave me my first kimonos, took me under his wing, and took me to tournaments with his children. He gave me an opportunity to grow up."

It was also through this coach that Aline was first introduced to wrestling. At first, she declined the offer to try it out—not knowing what her friends and family would think of the decision—but then her curiosity and competitive drive kicked in. When Aline was invited to compete at the Junior National Wrestling Championship, she did so out of a "taste for challenge." She was good at combat sports, and she just wanted to compete. Growing up as she did, Aline never imagined herself in this position, so when she stepped onto the national stage, she had to be her best. It was her past that drove her to create a better future, but it was always the present that gave her the opportunity to prove to herself and others that she was capable of overcoming the challenges that once pinned her down. "To mentally prepare for the matches," Aline says, "I always look at my opponents and try to imagine their lives, the difficulties they faced to be here. I'm sure that my opponents have had difficulties and challenges also. Everybody does, but I stand with my history, I stand with my background, and I say to myself 'I deserve to be here.'"

Aline had trained and was as prepared as she could be—nothing compared to the years to come, but for this moment she was ready. She went to the tournament, her first.

And she won it.

Aline became a national wrestling champion. This was the beginning of a new life, one she never could have imagined as a young girl running with the wrong crowd.

Thanks to the Brazilian Wrestling Confederation, Aline earned her spot on the team. Wrestling had opened its doors to her, and she eagerly raced through them, acquiring medals and taking her place on the champions' podium in tournament after tournament. Aline's eyes began to set on the ultimate prize—the Olympics.

The 2016 Summer Olympic Games were coming to Aline's home country of Brazil, in the city of Rio de Janeiro—Aline's hometown. All she had done for four years was wrestle, training longer and harder than she ever had before, eager for a chance to represent her country, in her home city, on the largest sporting stage in the world. She was disciplined and determined; nothing was going to stand in her way. After working towards her dream for so long, Aline made it a reality. She qualified for the Olympics.

Parading into the opening ceremonies with her Brazilian teammates, Aline could hardly believe her eyes."I made it," she kept repeating to herself. "I'm really here!" For Aline, Rio was an all-or-nothing event. She yearned to tell her story, to show people the change she hoped to see for Brazil's girls, and she knew winning a medal would elevate her voice to make this dream a reality. Aline felt the pressure weigh on her. "It was so heavy," she remembers.

As she stepped into the first match, she couldn't believe what she was seeing and hearing. Everyone was cheering, chanting her name, and singing a well-known song about being proud to be Brazilian. "There are no words to describe that feeling," she says.

Aline made it to the quarterfinals in the 75 kg class before being defeated by eventual bronze medalist Ekaterina Bukina from Russia. She was gutted, but what she remembers now, even more than the loss, is the overwhelmingly warm reaction from the crowd. "They stood up," she reminisces. "They applauded me. It was like the whole country was giving me a hug, and I needed it at that moment." Aline didn't come away from the Olympics with a medal, but she did leave with the love and respect of her fellow Brazilians. Vowing then to never give up on her dreams, she knew that Brazil was behind her.

Then, something unexpected happened, offering to change her life yet again.

Back in 2014, when Aline was training hard and dreaming of the Olympics, Dr. Sarah Hillyer and Dr. Ashleigh Huffman visited São Paulo to hold a women's empowerment workshop and follow up with Global Sports Mentoring Program (GSMP), alumnae—Paula Korsakas, Daniela Castro, and Casia Damani. Aline, who had become passionate about empowering girls through sport, attended the event and was awestruck. Here were two women, working as part of a global organization to do exactly what Aline had dreamed of doing. Aline was extremely impressed with Dr. Sarah, Dr. Ash, and the GSMP as a whole, and she knew she had to be a part of it. She remembers her conversation with Dr. Sarah, "For me, this program was an opportunity to learn how to empower more women through sports. I was already very passionate about the subject, but I didn't know how to do better, how to empower other women. When I went to talk to them after the event, Dr. Sarah said, 'I really love the way you talk about women's issues. I can see you're passionate about it, but, sadly, our program is only for those who speak English proficiently; otherwise, they won't enjoy the program and learn all that we hope they can.'"

Aline had lost other opportunities in her life because she didn't speak English, and she decided that she would not let it pin her down, again. After witnessing the incredible impact of the GSMP first-hand, she set her heart on one day becoming a part of this remarkable and innovative global sisterhood. Her fierce determination and relentless personal drive enabled her to tear down multiple barriers; she was not going to let a language barrier stop her. "I'll learn English," Aline vowed to Dr. Sarah, "and I'll apply for this program, because I really want to participate." At age 26, she set out to master the English language.

Aline had made up her mind, she just had to figure out how she was going to do it. "I don't think Dr. Sarah really thought I would learn English, because I was so focused on participating in the Olympics," she says. Since she was busy training

68

and also couldn't afford English tutoring or classes, Aline knew she needed to use her wrestler's fighting spirit to her advantage. She focused her attention on things she could control, rather than those she couldn't. One thing she could access was the Internet.

She created an account with Duolingo, a web-based platform that offers language learning free of charge. Already a world-class athlete, Aline knew the value of discipline and hard work, and she applied the same tenacity and dedication that she poured into preparing for the Olympics into learning English. In addition to her rigorous training, she was also using the Duolingo app, watching television series exclusively in English, and had a goal of learning at least three new words each day. In a relatively short period of time, Aline was speaking English.

Dr. Sarah was surprised while sorting through the tall stack of applications for the GSMP's 2017 class. There was Aline Silva's application, written in English. "I had to do my interview in English," Aline says, "and I could tell they were skeptical that I would be speaking proficiently in just three years, but I was!" After several rounds of virtual interviews, Aline earned her spot as one of only 17 GSMP participants.

Aline's pairing with mentor Julie Eddleman, and co-mentor Diane Cummins, was a winning combination. Julie is a former Global Client Partner at Google's Cincinnati location and a fierce champion for the visibility of women in all sectors, specifically targeting diversity in advertising. Like Aline, she believes that "one person or a small group of people can make an extraordinary difference."

In Brazil, Aline had never met a female executive, and she didn't know any women in business she could look to for advice. As an athlete, she had also never worked in a professional environment. "I didn't know little things. I didn't know how to talk or how I was supposed to dress," Aline recalled. Julie and Diane helped her with issues large and small, from learning how to dress professionally and speak in business settings to developing business plans, managing finances, and planning with the end goal in mind. The most important thing to emerge from this partnership for Aline, though, is Julie's continued encouragement. "I know every time I need her support she's there. Even when I don't realize I need her support, she's there for me!"

Aline dreamed of sharing the valuable life lessons she had learned through sports and how they helped her manage her emotions; she also hoped to make them a strength that worked for her, rather than against her. She wanted to help girls in Brazil learn English, knowing from experience that this would open countless doors. Julie was thrilled to work with Aline to devise a strong action plan, a guide that would help Aline use her platform as an Olympian to be a role model for Brazil's girls.

The result of this collaboration is Mempodera (Empower Me), a wrestling program for girls ages 6-15. This isn't just any wrestling program—it also demonstrates the power of education, with participants receiving free English classes as part of an extensive empowerment curriculum. Aline wants the girls of Brazil to learn to recognize opportunities, to see that they can be successful and achieve their goals. She teaches them that life is like sports—to win you must be disciplined, determined, and focused.

Even with all of the effort she had expended to get there, Aline's GSMP experience still surprised her. On the first day, when Dr. Sarah told her and the others that they would become sisters, Aline was skeptical. "I thought, okay, whatever. We're only here for five weeks," she says. "And then a couple of days in I found myself talking for hours into the night with five of my 'new sisters' about personal issues! That's something I never did before. We are truly sisters. It was a surprise, and it's such a gift."

Moreover, participating in the GSMP gave Aline an opportunity to take a step back from her professional wrestling career and reflect on how transformative sports really are. There is little doubt that sport truly saved her life. She started living in a safe and healthy way, a way that alcohol could never offer. Aline was now part of a global network working toward meaningful change, and her GSMP sisters gave her strength, sometimes even just as an encouraging voice in her head. "Wrestling is very sexist—it's easy to be affected by that," she says. "On tough days, when I want to cry and think everything is falling apart and I've messed it all up, I think of the challenges my sisters are facing. They aren't giving up. My sisters help me remember that I can't give up either."

When Aline walked into her Olympic matches in Rio, she believed wrestling was all she had. Because of the GSMP and the support of her sisters, she sees now that she's so much more than an athlete, and that losing a match doesn't define her worth.

"Look at where I came from," she proclaims. "I won't lose ever again. I can't. I love wrestling, but I know I can't lose. Every time I stand up to fight it's a win-win because I'm learning so much and helping to forge a path for others to follow."

Though her childhood was incredibly difficult, she believes that it is the source of her power. "That young girl in the streets gave me a different perspective on the world," Aline boldly states. "Now with my program, Mempodera, I look at my girls, and I know exactly how it is. I can tell them, 'I was in your place. I know how hard it is to face all these things.' I want them to learn to take responsibility for themselves in all aspects of their lives. 'You want something? Don't ask yourself if. Ask yourself how.'"

Sharing her experiences with Mempodera's youth, Aline emphasizes that obstacles, no matter how difficult, can be overcome. You just have to learn how to take them down.

71

JULIE EDDLEMAN'S TITLE IX EXPERIENCE

Julie Eddleman, who grew up in Indiana, first heard about Title IX in sixth grade. "The boys could go across the street during recess to play basketball," she recalled, "but school officials wouldn't let us join them. I didn't think that was very fair." Wanting to shoot hoops with the boys, Julie asked a teacher if she could play. One boy listening in complained, asking why she would make such a ridiculous request. "He was bullying me a bit," she confided, but her teacher, a basketball player, obtained permission for Julie and the boy in question to play at recess, mentioning the Title IX implications. She beat him. "For the rest of the school year, we got to go across the street and play basketball," she noted.

A swimmer and basketball player, Julie continued to hear about Title IX throughout junior high and high school. However, it was never recognized until her senior year in 1988, when the administration picked one person from each sport to honor. Her school's athletic director had a daughter, who attended college on an athletic scholarship, which Julie credits as the reason why there were so many opportunities for girls at her school to play sports.

Being an athlete helped Julie develop a variety of skills that are translatable to the non-sports world. Collaboration, knowing when to lead and also when to play a specific or supporting role, as well as how to connect and build a rapport with people—teammates or colleagues alike—are all valuable and desirable in today's workforce. "Those skills are incredibly transferable," Julie said. "We use them every day."

That's why, for Julie, the opportunity to develop such traits through sports and education should be accorded to everyone, regardless of where in the world they live. As social media and the Internet make the world smaller, more people learn about disparities and inequalities elsewhere. What many in the United States take for granted in Title IX is unique or unheard of in many countries. "We're all global citizens," she said. "It's our responsibility to use our privilege to fight for these opportunities."

"Sports are front and center in teaching leadership, when to lead, but also when to play a specific role. No matter if you are in business, in education, in an operating room, or running a nonprofit, it is critically important to bring out the best in your team."

DIANE CUMMINS' TITLE IX EXPERIENCE

Diane Cummins grew up on the cusp of Title IX. Just like her father, she played basketball; she also played soccer and ran track and field. She recalls how, once Title IX passed, a realm of possibility opened up. "It was a whole new world," she said. "I could play any sport I wanted to."

Being a high school athlete helped her physical and emotional development. "I gained so much confidence and sense of self at an earlier age than I would have had I not been able to play sports and compete," she confided. "It was critical to my growth as a human being."

Diane credits Title IX with planting the seed to attend Baylor University. She became a good runner after a dislocated shoulder injury forced her to temporarily halt basketball in high school. "Baylor was willing to look at me as a walk-on for track because it was a club sport at the time. I didn't end up doing it, but it opened the idea of possibility to me." She instead became the school's first women's basketball walk-on in 1981. "Title IX gave me that path," she said.

Moreover, college taught Diane that basketball was a door to much more than just a game. She learned leadership lessons, including how to use failures as fuel. "To this day, I don't have a fear of failure. I don't think I would have developed that resilience if I hadn't played sports and learned how to struggle."

Such lessons were clutch for when she entered the workforce after graduation. In her first job at Proctor & Gamble in 1985, she was one of just three women on her team, but she didn't let that intimidate her. She tapped into the lessons she learned on the basketball court and realized those leadership skills translated to the corporate world as well. "It made me feel like I could use my voice," she said.

"It was a lot easier for me to speak up for myself. They gave me a seat at the table early on because they could identify with me [as an athlete]."

Sports diplomacy is what happens when the sports world intersects with the actions of diplomacy: communication, representation, and negotiation. Traditionally, diplomacy was the purview of official state representatives—ambassadors, envoys, ministers, heads of state, and elite athletes. In today's globalized, Internet-connected world, non-state actors, citizens especially, increasingly participate in the conduct of diplomacy, which is often referred to as Public Diplomacy 2.0, through informal people-to-people exchanges. As a result, the nature of sports diplomacy and who conducts it has diversified as the line between diplomat and athlete has blurred.

Sports diplomacy has a long tradition. Since the Olympiads of ancient Greece, sport has been used as a tool for diplomacy and outreach, but the advent of organized international sports competition in the late nineteenth century—and their politicization after the First World War, notably by the Fascist governments of Italy and Germany—grew sport's import to the diplomatic realm. The Cold War was a crucible for sport's use as a tool of what Joseph Nye later coined "soft power," the ability to lead and persuade others to follow leadership thanks to the cultivation of a country's cultural ideals and values. As countries around the world sought out sports as a new battlefield terrain after 1945, women's sports and female athletes were increasingly brought into the mix.

Sporting victories and performances became more visible once widespread television broadcasts and satellite technology made Olympic and other major global sports events readily accessible to publics the world over. The power of images, especially on television, was enough to sway global public opinion.

This evolution coincided with the rise of the Sports Diplomacy and Sport for Development and Peace (SDP) fields and its emphasis on the promotion of peace and prosperity in the twenty-first century. Nelson Mandela famously stated in a 2000 speech that sport has the power to change the world. His remarks instigated more countries and organizations to think critically and seriously about sport's unique power beyond leisure and the business of entertainment. By 2003, the United Nations (UN) noted sport's contribution to diplomacy and education as well as its potential to help transform societies. Thus, the SDP field was officially recognized and entities of all sizes sought to create sport-based programming, devising strategies and carving out budgets that could sustain the novel intersection of sport and social innovation.

Today, SDP is a well-regarded field of theory and practice, and a growing list of proof points abound throughout this emerging sector, which further validate sport's legitimacy as a valuable tool. In the post-COVID-19 era, it is clear that the world needs innovative, inventive approaches to tackle the challenges global citizens face. That's why the Center for Sport, Peace, and Society's ability to deliver life-changing initiatives like the Global Sports Mentoring Program (GSMP) can unleash the exponential power of teamwork to move the metaphorical ball closer to the goal line and improve the ways sports are used to help countries work toward building more viable futures through the Sustainable Development Goals.

The GSMP is an example of this reimagination of sports diplomacy working in tandem with SDP to harness the power of sport and education in the fight for gender equality. It illustrates how intentionality can help nation-states and non-state sports actors reimagine how to better leverage the complementary approach of sports diplomacy. The experiences and lessons learned from GSMP, which focuses on UN Sustainable Development Goal (SDG) 5, Empowering Women and Girls demonstrates how sports diplomacy can help to organize, conceptualize, and strategize more coordinated efforts to address the SDGs.

Strong Women. Better World brings to life nine concrete examples of sport as a tool for social change in action. Through the stories, we hope readers will better understand the impact of the Center's work as well as the larger ability of sports diplomacy efforts, like the GSMP, to help make a difference in the people-to-people cultural, technical, and knowledge exchanges that are helping to spread Title IX's legacies well beyond U.S. borders.

"Integrity, authenticity, and productivity are the most important values I expect of myself and those under my leadership. I will lead by example."

NGA LE

Growing up in an era when it was practically unheard of for a Vietnamese woman to be on the business side of sports, Nga Le could never have imagined that this was where she would make her mark. In 2010, she graduated in the top five of her class from Vietnam's most prestigious school, the Foreign Trade University, with a bachelor's degree in international business administration. Upon graduation, Nga set out on her career path, driven to succeed as she had done in her academics.

Nga's professional career began as a personal assistant for tennis coach, Connor Nguyen, who opened Saigon Sports Academy (SSA), the first organization of its kind in Vietnam. SSA's mission is to help students not only practice sports skills but also develop comprehensively through three essential qualities in life: determination, steadfastness, and leadership. Though her inexperience in the sports industry created some initial doubts in her mind, Nga refused to let these uncertainties deter her, and she hit the ground running. To her own surprise, she excelled in this role. In their first year, SSA grew more quickly than they could have imagined, and, before long, Nga advanced quickly into an office manager position and then became head of marketing.

Everything in this world of sport was new and moving fast. In order to stay ahead of the game,

Nga put in countless hours studying the practicalities of the sports industry in order to make important strategic, financial, and legal decisions. In addition to her responsibilities at the academy, she was also busy co-founding the Saigon Heat, a men's professional basketball team, and the XLE Group, a sports entertainment company and another "first" in Vietnam. Breaking glass ceilings, Nga became the first woman on the private-sector side of sports to be named Chief of Staff.

"I'm thankful to be a Vietnamese woman," Nga says. "Compared to other countries in Asia, we have more rights and advantages." However, her society's patriarchal views still promoted traditional gender norms, notably in the sports sector. Nga watched in dismay as the men's teams were showered with media attention and accolades, even as the women's teams performed just as well—or better. Nga took notice of the glaring discrepancies in society's views towards female athletes.

Through her work, Nga recognized sport's tremendous potential to be a tool for character development. She fell in love with all sports, particularly basketball. It had been slow to take hold in Vietnam, but Nga enjoyed the game; the atmosphere surrounding it brought a sense of belonging, and she was introduced to the joy of teamwork. She began to think about basketball as a place where girls could also grow their confidence, strength, and leadership skills, if given the same opportunities as boys.

Nga strongly believed that Vietnamese women and girls deserved equal access, opportunities, and attention in all areas of sport. She knew that if women were more involved in sport, they would be better prepared to address the larger systemic issues. Nga's desire to help women in Vietnam grew stronger, but she didn't know where to start. "I searched for learning opportunities about women's empowerment," she remembers. "I actively looked for a mentor, and

I researched how to build people up and how to connect people within a team so they perform better than the sum of their parts. I wanted to change the mindsets of women so they felt empowered to play sports and be physically active."

Then, an opportunity for empowerment found her.

In 2015, Nga was selected as one of the 17 participants for the Global Sports Mentoring Program (GSMP) and was matched with two powerhouse women, Val Ackerman and Ann Wells Crandell. Val is the Commissioner of the Big East Conference, who had led the WNBA as its founding president, served on the board of the International Basketball Federation (FIBA), and was inducted into the Naismith Memorial Basketball Hall of Fame. Ann was Chief Marketing Officer at the Big East Conference at the time and has worked on marketing strategies for some of the best organizations in the world, both corporate and nonprofit. Nga's search for an empowering female mentor was over. "They gave me so much support," she says. "I learned a lot from them from a management standpoint, but I learned even more about life."

Though Nga didn't know how to elevate women's sports prior to the GSMP, participating in the program helped her think about ways she could use her position to advance opportunities for girls and women in Vietnam. Working with Val and Ann enabled Nga to narrow her focus on a more strategic plan of action. "You walk out of the program with something you're prepared to develop in your own country," Nga says. "It forces you to reflect and think about how you'll utilize your current platform to build something impactful for your community."

Furthermore, as Nga established connections with the others in the GSMP, who she would come to call "sisters", she reflected on her own identity as a Vietnamese woman. She realized that she would not be alone in her fight for equality and that when she feels overwhelmed, she has their encouragement and support.

"My sisters make me feel like I'm not alone in this journey," Nga says. "We understand each other and share similar values. We're like real sisters!"

Returning to Vietnam after the GSMP, Nga was well aware that changing the culture of women's sports would not be easy, but she was up for the challenge. She drew on her GSMP experience and the lessons learned from her mentors for strength. "I am a better version of myself," she says. "Integrity, authenticity, and productivity are the most important values I expect of myself and those under my leadership. I will lead by example."

Using all she had learned, from relationship building to marketing, Nga was ready to create change in Vietnam. In 2016, she launched She Will Be Strong (SWBS), a social enterprise created to inspire and provide a safe space for women to be physically and mentally healthy. SWBS organizes courses in yoga, dance, and self-defense for company employees; when these businesses purchase wellness courses, certified instructors deliver classes on-site, at the office, or a location chosen by the business. Well over half of the income generated from these courses goes to the Social Impact Fund, which supports pregnant single mothers and offers vocational training for victims of harassment and domestic violence. In partnership with other advocacy organizations, SWBS provides self-defense lessons and monthly financial support, to cover the cost of childbirth, for single mothers. Additionally, they also implement a Second Chance program to support single mothers and victims of violence and abuse. This program includes psychotherapy, vocational training, suitable job placement, and financial support if needed during apprenticeships. To date, SWBS has trained over 3,000 women and children, paid hospital fees for 20 pregnant women and provided monthly financial support to a shelter for homeless and pregnant single mothers.

Even though SWBS was thriving and assisting large numbers of women and girls, Nga was looking for ways to do even more. This desire was fueled into action after she read a report published by ActionAid and the Hanoi-based Institute for Social Development Studies, which stated that 60 percent of female adolescents reported experiencing sexual harassment at least once in their life. Needless to say, this didn't sit well with Nga. In response, SWBS partnered with the Ho Chi Minh City Taekwondo Federation to offer free self-defense classes for girls ages six and up. The class focused on introducing the psychology of self-defense, understanding the human body, and boosting self-confidence, giving women and girls the knowledge they need to protect themselves from would-be attackers.

According to Nga, her team in Vietnam is small but very passionate, dedicated, and capable. Currently, they are focusing on extending SWBS to Ho Chi Minh City and

Hanoi, with the hope of being financially sustainable in the next three years. Nga's dream for her organization doesn't stop there; she wants to impact the lives of one hundred thousand Vietnamese women and also envisions other Asian countries establishing their own self-sustaining chapters of SWBS. While this sounds ambitious, Nga is confident that the lessons she learned from the GSMP—especially the importance of connecting with like-minded people—will help her to reach this goal.

Prior to the GSMP, Nga didn't think her career or accomplishments were anything special. She didn't realize the importance of what she was achieving as the "first" in so many areas; she was just doing what she knew in her heart to be right. When she arrived in the U.S. for the GSMP and heard her sisters from around the world speak of their challenges, realities, and responsive actions to overcome deep-seated discrimination, she realized she, too, was living under the same conditions. Because

living in this reality was all she ever knew, she never thought about the absence of women in the sports industry as a gender equality issue. Nga had gained a global perspective complete with new knowledge, tools, and networks that enabled her to take more intentional action.

Now, whenever Nga addresses Vietnam's girls, she never fails to remind them that a strong woman is independent, confident, and true to herself. A strong woman brings positive energy to people around her, owns her destiny, and is brave enough to pursue her dreams. Nga uses her own life to illustrate this as well as the lessons learned from her GSMP experience and sisters. Having inspiring mentors changed Nga's life, and she never misses an opportunity to pass this advice on to Vietnam's girls. "Critics said, 'You have no career path,'" she recalls. "'You're not going to earn a lot of money, plus there are no positions out there for Vietnamese women in sports.' But, I am proof that women can make a

good living in sport. I'm here, so why can't other women do it too?"

In 2017, Nga partnered with NBA Asia to create a special project aimed at providing basketball training for all physical education teachers in the country. This partnership resulted in basketball being recognized as an official sport in the Vietnam education system. In the same year, she became the first-ever female Chief Executive Officer (CEO) of the Vietnam Basketball Association (VBA), where she managed a staff of 30 people, reported to team owners, and managed the league's Board of Directors.

Having been promoted to CEO, the responsibilities, workload, and political challenges were starting to get the better of her. Her time was consumed with all of the obligations of managing an organization, from cultivating relationships to earning sponsorships, while simultaneously struggling to gain the respect of male executives. Nga was completely overwhelmed and ready to quit. She knew that if anyone could understand her situation, it would be her mentor, Val—after all, Val was often the only woman in a room full of men and one of only a handful of female executives in the international basketball landscape. "I reached out to Val," Nga recalls, "and she immediately emailed me back and advised me. I still have her email and read it when I need encouragement. She gave me the spirit to continue on with what I'm doing because she's been through the same thing. I look at her and think 'someday I'll be like that.'"

Through her representation as a female executive, Nga is already a strong force in Vietnam. She stands firm in her conviction that women and girls should have the autonomy to make decisions for their own lives, bodies, and happiness. Dedicated to eliminating gender disparities in her country, Nga is creating better opportunities for future generations.

VAL ACKERMAN'S TITLE IX EXPERIENCE

Val Ackerman grew up playing basketball and was an early beneficiary of one of the first athletic scholarships given by the University of Virginia under Title IX. "It really transformed my educational experience," she recalled. Playing basketball at Virginia was a vital opportunity to also obtain the life skills that come out of playing sports, being part of a team, and representing her university. "I was so proud to go to UVA and play sports there," she said.

It was a time of female pioneers as Title IX provisions were implemented in the mid-to-late 1970s. While there were increased opportunities for women to play basketball at the collegiate level, playing the sport at the elite international level did not become a reality for women until 1976, when the Montreal Summer Games held the first women's Olympic basketball tournament.

Val was intimately aware of Title IX and its ability to change women's experiences, but marveled at how far women's sports have come some 50 years later. "Look how many athletes have come out of that experience and have gone on to do important things with their lives, in part because they had the benefit of that educational experience that Title IX made possible," she said.

That's why, for Val, it is critical to re-educate the general public about the law, how it benefits high school and collegiate athletics programs, and its legacy. "Equity, advancement, the achievement of women everywhere," she said, "that's what this sports experience can do in women's formative years in terms of building the life skills and life profiles for them to go on and do great things in other fields."

Val emphasized that it's equally important to educate the world about the myriad ways that societies benefit from women who have the chance to play sports as part of their overall education. "I take a lot of pride in how historically the U.S. has been seen as a beacon and a model," she said of Title IX's results and how they've helped to make U.S. basketball a leading international figure in terms of women in and around the game.

That's why Val views it as vital that U.S. women help arm their international counterparts to work towards the concept of a global Title IX. Similar legislation could ensure that women and girls have equal access to play sports as part of their education.

"We need a campaign for a global Title IX that requires equitable resources, so that educational opportunities are made available and women and girls have a chance to play sports. This would help women sit more generally in society, because sports and women and societal advancement are all linked."

"Always pursue your dreams, especially if it's something that makes you happy. Just because some parts of society may be against it, it doesn't mean that you're wrong."

RABA'A AL HAJERI

Raba'a Al Hajeri was raised in a community where traditions and family were of primary importance, and she grew up wanting to make her parents happy. She also loved physical activity, and throughout grade school, she played every sport she could. One of her favorite sports was soccer, which she grew up playing in the street, eventually landing a spot on her college team. She says, "I played soccer because I wanted to run and have my run be with a purpose—passing, shooting, tackling."

In Kuwait, sports and opportunities to participate in them were seemingly everywhere; however, traditional gender roles were strong in the country, too. "Every residential area has sports clubs," Raba'a explains, "and there's nothing in the constitution that says girls cannot join them." Yet, sometimes tradition outweighs even the law; men continued to close the door to women, questioning why they would want to join in the first place. As a girl, Raba'a remembers going to a swimming pool each day at 5 a.m.

"I want to swim," she would say.

"It's only for men," the attendant would reply.

"Where does it say that?" asked Raba'a. "There's nothing in the rules. You can't stop me."

"Because you're a girl," he said. "Someone might look from the window."

"Why is that my problem?" she would ask in exasperation.

"Tradition, unfortunately, became so ingrained in the way we do things, that people assumed it was a rule that girls can't do this or that," Raba'a explains. "From the 1970s till now, women's sports lost their value." Raba'a was growing weary of being ruled by tradition. She began to realize that she didn't share the cultural beliefs that kept women from doing what they loved, and she wanted to discover the world from her own perspective.

Raba'a remembers the exact moment that led her on a new path to self-discovery and women's empowerment.

She was conducting an interview as the editor of a student magazine, but this wasn't her dream job; she was an athlete, not a journalist. She had not been able to find her footing in the sports world. On this particular day, she was talking to Ahmed Al Majed, one of Kuwait's first triathletes. She asked him, "What's it like competing in three different sports during a single race? How did you get into the sport?"

Ahmed reached into his wallet and took out a picture.

"This is me before I began training and competing in triathlons," he said, pointing to an out of shape version of himself. Raba'a was mesmerized; she couldn't believe the transformation from the image in the photo to the bubbly, energetic athlete standing before her. Ahmed told Raba'a his story of how he began cycling and running to improve his overall health and well-being. Through his newfound interest, Ahmed became the owner of Extreme Sports, a retail and distribution company that specializes in action and endurance sports, and was working toward a master's degree in sports management. Sports had changed his whole life, and he was following his passion.

He must have sensed Raba'a's awe and excitement.

"You can do it, too," he said. "I'll give you a bike and train you for the next race, if you want to compete."

Raba'a didn't know then how this interaction would profoundly change her life and alter the landscape of women's sports in Kuwait.

In 2010, after one year of intense training, Ahmed recommended Raba'a compete in the Barcelona triathlon. Barcelona was 3,590 miles away, and a nine-hour flight from Kuwait, but Ahmed knew that it would be a good starting point for Raba'a; it was a beginner-friendly race and the weather was similar to the conditions she had been training in. Raba'a readily accepted his recommendation and traveled to Barcelona to compete in her first triathlon.

The event was transformative.

Raba'a explains, "Before competing in this race, I led a very different life, more sedentary and too comfortable. I lacked a challenge and goal to excite my life journey." This one race led Raba'a to pursue more athletic endeavors and helped reignite her love for sports in general. She affirms that triathlon changed her entire career, as she moved from journalism to sports. On the plane back to Kuwait after the race, Raba'a knew she was hooked. She turned to her trainer and spoke her dream aloud for the first time: "I don't want to work at the magazine anymore," she said. "I'm going to start a triathlon club."

Very soon after returning home, Raba'a and Ahmed

founded The 3 Club to promote national interest for the sport. For the next four years, Raba'a became immersed in the multi-sport race, training herself and others to compete internationally. However, Kuwait didn't yet have the infrastructure to support her endeavor, corporations weren't interested in sponsoring their club, and the athletes grew restless when they didn't have the resources to get the team to races. This forced Raba'a to make the difficult decision to close The 3 Club in 2014.

Thankfully, that failed business venture didn't cause her to drown in despair—it actually had the opposite effect—Raba'a was more positive and driven than ever. Agreeing to compete in a triathlon had changed everything for her. Now, she looked for more opportunities to say yes, feeling that it could only move her forward. "Every time I say yes, good things happen for me," she says. "I used to be scared. I had an 'I can't' mentality. Breaking away from that mindset gave me so much empowerment and motivation. It gave me the sense that I'm on an adventure."

Even though her first sports business undertaking wasn't successful, Raba'a credits the failure of The 3 Club for her next endeavor. In 2014, two of her friends who loved CrossFit wanted to start a new socially-driven company and asked her to be part of the start-up. She said yes.

They agreed the company should focus on community, solving problems through sports, and empowering women. They called it Eighty Percent, based on the "80-20 rule," which suggests prioritizing the 20% of factors that will produce the best results. Therefore, they would focus on the issues in Kuwait they felt certain could be solved using sports. The primary issues they wanted to address were the lack of investment and resources for women's sports and the need for creative programming that enabled communities to be more active. "The mission at Eighty Percent is to create and execute socially impactful events, programs, and initiatives that elevate the standard of events in Kuwait as well as inspire our participants to adopt healthier lifestyles." Once the organization had a name, a plan, and a mission statement, the next step was to host their first event.

Raba'a knew that many women and girls wanted to play soccer but were cautioned against participating in a "man's sport". To combat this, she and her team at Eighty Percent created a safe environment through their inaugural women's soccer tournament. Over 16 teams registered for the local event. Some were already established, coming from local clubs, academies, and schools. However, many teams were formed of individual applicants who just wanted to play. Raba'a and her colleagues divided the individuals into teams and trained them before the tournament. "We acquired fields and hired private coaches," she says. "There were girls who had never played before, because they were scared, but they came and we trained them. They were smiling from ear to ear."

The following year, this same team had its own coach, its own uniforms, and a sponsor. They have since played in all of Eighty Percent's tournaments, even spawning some of their own soccer academies. As of now, Eighty Percent has received sponsorships from over 240 companies over the course of eight years; they average four private sector sponsors and two public sector sponsors per event. It's safe to say that they are successfully living up to their slogan, "collaborating for change."

Raba'a had known from the start that women's soccer could be bigger in Kuwait than it was. "We wanted better facilities, funding, and sponsors. Why should we sit and complain when we can do something about it?" Refusing to let patriarchal, traditional thinking break their momentum, Eighty Percent pushed forward, attracting new sponsors from Kuwait's public and private sectors. They also found international sources, one of which is La Liga, the men's top professional soccer division of the Spanish Football League System. By not taking no for an answer, Raba'a was able to garner this kind of support.

With all that Raba'a has done for the women of Kuwait, it was clear that she would be an outstanding fit for the Global Sports Mentoring Program (GSMP) class of 2019. She was mentored by Liz Gray, Head of Cultural and Consumer Insights at Creative Artists Agency in New York City. On the first day of the program, Liz made Raba'a a promise. She said, "I will make sure that you learn anything and everything you want." In turn, Raba'a made the most of her time with Liz in NYC, absorbing all she could. "The experience was very rich," she says. "I had the opportunity to learn from professionals who had invested years toward the same goals I aspire to achieve." During the second half of the program, Raba'a found immense power in connecting with a community of women who were fighting the same battles in their own countries. Raba'a took her newfound insights, the support of her mentor, and an amazing network of women home to Kuwait, ready to implement change.

Raba'a has never lacked perseverance, but the GSMP experience increased her drive to overcome the obstacles standing in her way. "When people say no to me, I'm even more determined to get a yes. I'll make it my life's focus to get a yes. Even in Kuwait, when people say no to me, I say 'okay—you say no now, but I'm gonna get this eventually, even if I have to wait ten years, I'm gonna get it.'"

In September 2019, Raba'a became an Assistant Secretary General of the Kuwait Triathlon Federation (KTF), only the second woman ever to be elected to the board of a sports federation in Kuwait. In this role, she ensures that youth, women, and all club athletes have equal and ample opportunities to train, compete, and progress in triathlon. She also serves as the head of KTF's Technical Com-

mittee. Raba'a is creating new opportunities for women and girls, working to guarantee that what happened to her doesn't happen to the next generation of athletes.

Things are changing in Kuwait, thanks to Raba'a and her colleagues, and now has a committee whose mission is to reform women's sports. This group uses their combined influence to remind authorities that to participate in the Olympics, they must let women practice their craft. Raba'a knows there is still progress to be made, because women continue to be put in a predefined box. She says, "We need to empower women and girls so the next generation is well-informed about what is okay and what is not, and to not let men decide what we can and cannot do." Raba'a also wants to educate Kuwait's men so that the culture can move away from the constant objectification of women.

Raba'a is driven by a passion for helping others and doing good in the world. To this end, she uses her platform at Eighty Percent and her incredible success at the highest levels of Kuwaiti sport and is always on the hunt for like-minded individuals looking to make a difference. "When we work together, we all succeed faster and become better," she proclaims. "This is not about one person; it's about a group of people fixing something in our own country so others can benefit."

The most important lesson Raba'a wants to instill is to focus on one thing you can do to create opportunities, instead of the external factors that have dictated your life.

"Never take no for an answer," she says. "Always pursue your dreams, especially if it's something that makes you happy. Just because some parts of society may be against it, it doesn't mean that you're wrong."

With her positivity, never-quit attitude, and business savvy, Raba'a will never waiver in her commitment to empower Kuwaiti women and girls through sport.

LIZ GRAY'S TITLE IX EXPERIENCE

Liz Gray grew up playing a variety of sports, including tennis and basketball, but she particularly excelled at running. "Growing up, I took sports for granted, but in hindsight recognized the important role they had on my life, whether it was through new places, opportunities, or relationships," she said.

Serving as president of her high school's athletic council provided Liz's first taste of empowerment. "They gave me a voice, that was crucial," she recalled of the role and how it taught her different skills, including goal setting and resilience.

Liz was part of a generation in which Title IX made playing sports during college a normal activity, even though she opted not to participate when she went to the University of Richmond. All the same, it wasn't until later in her professional career that Liz realized just how powerful a role sports play in girls' education and future success in life.

"When we look at how many girls who played sports in high school go on to become executives, it's ridiculous," she said of research by Ernst & Young that found 94% of female C-suite executives and 80% of Fortune 500 female executives play(ed) sports. This data illustrates the direct correlation between sports participation and business leadership. "That's when Title IX's sports provisions really became significant to me."

At work, Liz has witnessed firsthand how women who were athletes in high school or college go on to impact the professional realm. "It's pretty powerful," she noted of how female colleagues deploy the skills learned on the field in a business setting. The issue remains that there's not enough being done today to keep girls playing sports at all levels.

For Liz, that's why re-educating people about Title IX, and the long-term benefits it provides individuals and society at large, is so critical. "Sport is just the tool to address a huge cultural crisis that still exists," she said. "We have to look at sports as a solution, not only to give women opportunities to play—and play at a high level—but to solve other cultural issues and drive financial growth."

It's an opportunity to restart the conversation, to learn lessons from progress, and to better understand the importance of the legislation's longer-term impacts at home and globally. "As Americans, leading in some of these important conversations has never been more important," Liz emphasized. "Fifty years later, we can comfortably say there has been an economic benefit to Title IX's sports provisions. Today, we can look back and say, 'look at the domino effect this has had on our economy.' So, let's look at female athletes and the roles they go on to fill."

"Title IX is an overwhelming example of leading the way in what's possible when working towards equality. Plus, sports play a role in driving important cultural conversations forward."

The Global Sports Mentoring Program (GSMP) was created in 2012, championed by then-Secretary of State Hillary Rodham Clinton, herself a pioneer for women's empowerment and equal opportunity, as the flagship component of the Department's Empowering Women and Girls through Sports initiative (EWGS). The GSMP became the newest addition to a growing SportsUnited portfolio and the first to partner with a private-sector media company, espnW. Although far from the first sports diplomacy push, this was the cumulation of nearly a decade's worth of increased attention given to sports as part of larger public and cultural diplomacy endeavors.

Today, GSMP: Empowering Women through Sports is a five-week immersive mentorship program that aims to empower international delegates to serve their local communities by increasing opportunities for women and girls to participate in sports. Each fall, approximately 17 women who demonstrate leadership skills and have experience in the sports sector are chosen from a list of nominees selected by U.S. Embassies across the world. These mentees are typically between 25 and 40 years of age, proficient in the English language, and have three or more years of work or volunteer experience within the sport sector.

Tapping into the unique power of mentoring, host organizations and mentors from the corporate and non-profit worlds are chosen to work alongside mentees during an intensive three-week period in the United States. Mentors provide delegates with opportunities to cultivate management and business skills in an American sports environment and help shape their vision for social change. As a part of the nomination process, each delegate identifies a key need or challenge facing women and girls in her home country.

During the mentorship, each mentee develops a detailed action plan to address this challenge through sports-based initiatives and innovations. All action plans are designed to be implemented upon the mentees' return home and share the common goal of creating sports opportunities for underserved and disadvantaged populations. Development of the action plan and presenting it to peers, mentors, program partners, and members of the U.S. Department of State serves as the culmination of the U.S.-based mentorship experience. Since 2012, 83% of GSMP alumnae have implemented at least one phase of their action plans focused on using sport to empower women and promote gender equality.

The GSMP is also a technical exchange between and among participants, one of its notable distinction points. The exchanges that occur between mentors and mentees facilitates knowledge transfer of different sports models and industry approaches, and also deepens understanding of other countries and their cultures.

Moreover, although the program is a bilateral sports diplomacy initiative, the GSMP experience fosters a more multilateral engagement and form of sports diplomacy.

Thus, the GSMP passes along the benefits of Title IX's gains to women and girls around the world, so that they don't have to start from scratch in the race towards gender equity and equality.

The GSMP was conceptualized within the context of Title IX's long-term legacies. There's a clear correlation between women's participation in sports and the boardroom: 94% of female C-suite executives and 80% of Fortune 500 female executives play(ed) sports, according to Ernest & Young, showing a direct correlation between sports participation and business leadership. The GSMP embodies this calculus, seeking to share the lessons and benefits of Title IX with others worldwide. Since its inception a decade ago, the program has created a ripple effect with alumnae taking the lessons they've learned, the networks they've built, and the skills they've cultivated to empower marginalized communities around the world.

To date, the Center for Sport, Peace, and Society has worked with more than 100 mentors to train 144 GSMP sisters from 67 countries who have: founded 154 new sport-based organizations aimed at using sport as a tool to empower women, girls; impacted some 341,741 participants; mobilized 8,589 new volunteers; and established 2,072 new local and global partnerships.

It's a strong start, and the Center strives to work with many more advocates around the world to help unlock their potential in the fight for gender equality. Through a sports diplomacy initiative like the GSMP, the Center is helping to create more Title IX moments and stronger, more resilient communities for all.

"Now I know very well how to run life's marathon, how to stay consistent and go through the pain knowing that I can endure it."

NOORALHUDA **DAJANI**

Jordan

Nooralhuda Dajani (Noor) was born with a love of physical activity. She spent hours kicking a soccer ball, hitting a tennis ball against the wall, and practicing Taekwondo kicks, imagining herself representing Jordan as an Olympic athlete one day. Her parents encouraged Noor and her seven sisters to be active, and they provided enough space in their home for them to do so. Though her parents were supportive of this in the confines of the family home, traditional patriarchal attitudes about women playing sports in her country were not changing fast enough for Noor. Too young to advocate for herself, she became convinced that her dream may not come to fruition.

After several unsuccessful attempts to establish her identity as an athlete, Noor gave up fighting for herself and resigned to meet society's expectations. "The only freedoms for women were within the boundaries of religious and cultural expectations of women," she says. Being an athlete required her to train publicly around men, which wasn't allowed. "At some point," she says, "I stopped thinking about the restrictions and just took it as 'this is my life—this is fact.' I just went hiding inside of myself and chose to look away." From age 12 until 25, Noor struggled with the weight of a disappointment that seemed too heavy to lift.

Fulfilling cultural gender norms of being a wife and mother, Noor married her husband, Obada, at 25, and gave birth to their first child shortly after. Mothers are expected to sacrifice their own dreams and aspirations for their families, but Noor wanted more for herself. "I trusted that Obada was the kind of man who would hold me tight and set me free at the same time." Noor began a journey of self-discovery, gradually building more awareness around who she was and wanted to be. She searched to find what made her happy outside of her role in the family, and her mind continued to focus back on memories of playing sports as a child. Noor rediscovered her identity as an athlete and decided then that nothing would stop her from playing sports. Obada understood Noor's passions and was incredibly supportive of her decision.

When Obada was awarded a Fulbright fellowship, Noor and her family moved to Ohio. It was during this two-year stay in the United States that Noor was able to be away from the constant reminders of her country's societal limitations. Here, she had the chance to discover her true self, the athlete, and live the life she had always envisioned. With educational resources and certification opportunities more accessible and well-developed in the U.S., Noor grew more in the fitness space than she ever would have been able to at home.

Noor's fitness training in the U.S. came with some challenges, however. As a Middle Eastern woman who wore a hijab, she faced constant discrimination in and out of the gym. "It wasn't always easy," Noor remembers. "Being a hijabi in the

United States, in an industry that is obsessed with the body, was difficult. I sometimes was looked down upon and had to work hard to prove that I had what it takes to belong in this space and that it was my passion." Knowing this opportunity would end once she moved back to Jordan, Noor focused on individual sports which she could practice in any gym and compete at a local level without needing to join a club or federation. She kept her sights set on obtaining certifications in Spinning, TRX®, boot camp training, personal training, CrossFit®, and Olympic weightlifting.

Through family-like support within the CrossFit community, Noor was able to mine her inner strengths and her confidence began to soar. "I met some amazing people who were supportive and celebrated with me each step of the way," she says. She was finally discovering the freedom she always wanted, and now she was ready to help Jordanian women and girls find their own. She was stronger now, both physically and mentally, and determined to continue doing what she loved, regardless of society's expectations. This mindset propelled Noor to become the first CrossFit Level 3 Trainer in Jordan and the first woman to do so in the Middle East. "I really like to coach and help people move and feel better," Noor says. She was committed to providing fitness training to Jordanian women and girls, so she bought her

She had a Dream ...

own equipment and started training people from her home.

Noor founded MePower, a dual physical exercise and mental health program, with the goal of training women who wanted the intensity of CrossFit without the heavy weight-lifting. Her organization aims to empower women by building strength, confidence, and resilience. Until 2019, MePower was in an experimental and developmental phase. Noor began to recognize the connections between mental toughness and determination of female athletes built inside the gym and their ability to translate those skills into real-world settings. This proved to Noor that she was doing something beneficial for Jordan's women and girls beyond the four walls of a gym. However, she still wondered how to grow the impact while sustaining the long-term vision.

The answer for Noor came after she applied to participate in the 2019 Global Sports Mentoring Program (GSMP) and was selected as one of only 17 women. The thought of leaving her family for five weeks to attend weighed heavily on Noor's mind, but Obada was more optimistic. "This is the time for you to focus on your dreams," he reassured her. "We'll find a way to make it all work."

Noor was partnered with the head of Global Brand Communications for New Balance, Romina Bongiovanni. They spent three weeks at the New Balance headquarters in Boston, working to re-engineer Me-Power's programs, narrow its focus, and develop a marketing plan. "The whole mentoring team was super helpful and engaging," Noor says. "They helped me refine my business strategy to maximize MePower's impact on women in Jordan. Participating in the GSMP was also a chance to reset my priorities and to understand that I am part of something bigger." At the end of the five week program, Noor had gained a cheering section full of mentors as well as a global sisterhood of fellow GSMP participants. There was no doubt left in her mind that she was on the right path, and she was even more motivated to use sport to build resilience, self-awareness and confidence in Jordan's women.

Two months prior to Noor's arrival to the United States, Romina informed Noor that part of her mentorship would take place in New York during the city's annual Marathon. "Can I run in it?" Noor excitedly asked. "Can you get me in?" Always one to challenge herself, Noor knew this was a once-in-a-lifetime opportunity to run in one of the most renowned marathons in the world. Romina said yes, she could get her in the race. Though many people train for years before ever attempting a marathon, Noor had only eight weeks to prepare.

"On the day of the race, I knew I wasn't ready physically," she remembers, "but I knew that mentally I could do it. I just needed to put one foot in front of the other for 26.2 miles." It took Noor nearly six hours of running without stopping, which

she found painful and exhausting but also meditative. Noor powered through the discomfort, running the fastest pace during the last mile. When she made it through the finish line, she burst into tears. Finishing was another turning point in her life. "Now I know very well how to run life's marathon," she says, "how to stay consistent and go through the pain knowing that I can endure it. All I have to do is not let my mind trick me into choosing the path of least resistance."

Two weeks after Noor returned to Jordan, her father passed away. Putting all she learned during the GSMP on the line, Noor powered through the pain and began organizing MePower's first seminar, focusing on building resilience through fitness. The women who attended the seminar looked to Noor for guidance. At the end of the workshop, the last day before Jordan closed down due to COVID-19 restrictions, one woman confided in Noor. "This was life-changing for me," she said. "My whole mindset has changed. I approach physical activity, self-care, and life conflicts differently now." Noor realizes that changing the world for women and girls in her country is going to take more time and hard work, but the success of the first workshop will serve as a constant reminder that she is helping Jordan's women live beyond the constraint of cultural gender norms.

Today, Noor is a CrossFit and Olympic weightlifting coach who sees participation in sports as the key to unlocking human potential. For her, it is a kind of medita-tion, self-actualization and a rehearsal for life's hardships, which inspired her to co-author the book, Empowering Women through Healthy Living—Jordan, in 2020. She is a role model for women and girls in her community and aspires to instill in them the courage to follow their dreams. Noor has shattered many glass ceilings in her country, but she's not finished. She still dreams of one day competing at the Olympics and will never stop doing the heavy lifting for women and girls in Jordan.

ROMINA BONGIOVANNI'S TITLE IX EXPERIENCE

Romina Bongiovanni knows first-hand how Title IX created a ripple effect of consciousness and equality in sports, way beyond the geographic bounds of its legislation. Growing up in Argentina, she saw how Title IX ignited a much-needed conversation about women and girls in sports as a general concept, even if equality wasn't yet achieved.

As a young girl in Buenos Aires, Romina admired the talent and strength of her hometown hero and tennis champion, Gabriela Sabatini. The star's genuineness and poise during TV interviews struck a chord. "That's probably when I first became aware of the importance of Title IX and its power in women seeing themselves represented at the largest sporting events around the world," she said.

Romina played tennis, volleyball, and handball, driven by a desire for growth and betterment. Playing sports was invaluable, even though she initially only pursued them out of enjoyment, because they taught her resilience, collaboration, and commitment. They also helped to develop confidence in herself, a trait that Romina leaned on after moving to the United States and embarking on a career in communications.

Given her international background, Romina points to the importance of Title IX for women and girls everywhere. "The United States sets the tone for the rules and regulations of global sports, empowering social and economic growth," she noted. "In the past fifty years, Title IX hasn't just empowered athletes, it has influenced and shaped stories, dreams, and aspirations of generations of women and girls worldwide."

That's why Romina firmly advocates for a form of Title IX globally. "We need a worldwide effort," she said, "a policy to mandate that there are more—and equal—opportunities for women and girls to play sports. This is important because it will inspire and result in more female sports anchors, coaches, professional athletes, executives, and referees as role models, but also well-balanced participation in school sports and equal funding and sponsorships for all, not just girls."

Being part of the GSMP family has been both rewarding and illuminating for Romina. "I'm grateful for and conscious that the impact and advocacy created by Title IX led us to our own success, to finding more open doors, fewer barriers, and to being more intentional team players for one another as a way to pay it back," she said. "It's those moments when we first meet a new GSMP class, when we gather to champion the action plans from incredible sisters, and many more times in between, that we, as women, lift each other up and truly honor the legacy of Title IX."

"Female athletes, as well as women in corporate leadership positions, might still be outnumbered by our male counterparts today, but playing sports has a very tangible, long-lasting effect on women that we take with us off the field and into the workplace, our homes, and in nurturing our relationships. The lessons of playing sports are endless and live at the intersection of knowing yourself and a continued quest for authenticity in all areas of life."

CONCLUSION

Sport has the ability to bridge divides, unite communities, and promote inclusion. Allowing girls equal access to sports is proven to have significant effects both inside and outside the sporting arena. Studies continue to show that women who participate in sports suffer fewer health problems, have more self-confidence, and experience greater social and economic mobility. Title IX pushed the United States toward equalizing women's rights and laid the foundation for generations of women across the globe to benefit from the beauty of sport.

Fifty years after Title IX packed the first punch in the fight for gender equality, there remains much work to be done, both in the United States as well as worldwide. Women and girls face severe inequalities, without opportunities or access to play sports and reap its benefits, and remain underrepresented in sport-based careers. Moreover, female change-makers lack structural and financial support for their initiatives aimed at empowering their communities through sport.

The power of individuals to affect change cannot be underestimated. Just take the example of Pat Summitt and the basketball-playing girls in Sulaymaniyah, Iraq. That hoops program grew from 60 young athletes in 2007 to more than 450 today who operate out of a brand new facility, never miss a practice, and always sit in the first three rows of every classroom they enter. They, too, honor the lessons of Coach Summitt. "I will follow Pat Summitt's path to raise a better and healthier generation," says Khoshee, one of the 15 Iraqi girls who met Summit in 2009. "I will become her legacy."

Each of us can leave a legacy, too.

Knowing the benefits of sports participation for women and girls, it's essential that we take the necessary steps in providing them with opportunities to reach their full potential. Join the Center for Sport, Peace, and Society in strengthening social ties and enhancing our shared humanity through sport. Together we can build opportunities for female voices and women in sports, now and in the future.

JOIN THE TEAM

We believe social change is a team sport! Use this QR code to learn how you can join the team and help us support more heroes like lina, Carla, Po-Chun, Ashreen, Cynthia, Aline, Nga, Raba'a, and Noor—nine strong women you already know using the power of sport and education to create a more equitable, inclusive, and peaceful world.

SOCIOPOLITICAL CONTEXT

In this bonus chapter, you'll find helpful sociopolitical
and historical information of the countries featured in
this book. It is our hope that this context will shed greater
light on the significance of the GSMP sisters' work. Be
sure to visit our website, where you will find research and
historical data for the 67 countries in which our 144 sisters are working to use sports to advance women's rights.

NORTH MACEDONIA - HOME OF ILINA ARSOVA

The Republic of North Macedonia is a small, land-locked country nestled in the mountainous southeastern Balkans. From 1945 until its September 1991 declaration of independence, it was one of six republics that constituted the Federal People's Republic of Yugoslavia.

Throughout the Cold War, Yugoslavia danced a tenuous line between the Soviet-led Eastern Bloc communist states and the U.S.-led capitalist countries of the West. Cultural endeavors, such as sports, remained more in line with the socialist-centric concept of prioritizing the good of the community, and the country, over the individual. Team sports like soccer, basketball, and volleyball were highly regarded, wildly popular, and helped create a sense of unity and belonging. This is an important consideration given the many different cultures and peoples of the Balkans.

A few individual sports were also popular. Some disciplines like skiing and mountaineering were part of physical education programs in other parts of Yugoslavia, but not so much in North Macedonia, where mountain climbing gradually became more popular due to tourism in the 1970s. Even then, mountain climbing remained a sport dominated by men, thanks to ingrained ideas of masculinity and the sport's longtime use in military training.

Around the same time, however, the feminist movement began to change social norms and cultural conceptions of what women could do. Until the 1970's, sports were increasingly part of this conversation for many opinion-makers and cultural elites, who thought certain sports, such as soccer and mountaineering, were unsuitable for women and at odds with their ideals of femininity.

MEXICO—HOME OF CARLA BUSTAMANTE

The status quo in Mexico resulted in political, economic, and social stagnation, and reform had become necessary. Although the government pushed new economic development initiatives in the late 1980s and early 1990s, the continued one-party rule by the Partido Revolucionario Institucional (PRI), or Institutional Revolutionary Party, in power since 1929, floundered and ultimately paved the way for multi-party democratic elections in 2000.

Meaningful change was much slower to occur in society's attitudes toward women. The 1917 Constitution, a product of the Mexican Revolution, recognized the need to elevate women's work, stipulated maternity leave for working mothers, and promoted equal pay. Yet, there remained deep divisions in society's ideas about what constituted women's work, which was still defined mainly within the domestic spheres, while men dominated all areas of public life.

Much of this was reflected in Mexican society's attitudes towards women in sports. As in many other countries, modern sports were introduced there in the late nineteenth century.

For a short time, baseball was Mexico's national sport, though it didn't truly begin building steam until the 1880s. It was popular with American expatriates, soldiers, and Mexico's exiled Cuban communities and was spreading quickly. The country's first professional baseball league, established in the 1920s, featured players from Cuba and the U.S. Negro League. Baseball's dominance in Mexico would be short-lived, quashed by soccer in the 1950s.

Soccer's prominent role in Mexican society coincided with evolving attitudes about women in sports. In 1970, the Italian company Martini & Rossi sponsored the first unofficial Women's World Cup soccer tournament in Italy. The Mexican team captured hearts and won third place, leading to heavy promotion in the national media and a tournament the following year played in Mexico City and Guadalajara. The final match between Mexico and Denmark in 1971 drew some 110,000 fans to Mexico City's Azteca Stadium, a world record in women's sport. It earned glowing media coverage, but women's soccer in Mexico languished, and it would be another 20 years before the first official FIFA Women's World Cup.

Despite the willingness of the press to champion women's sports, if only briefly, women who wished to forge a career in sports media faced a daunting uphill battle. Though the media had proven that they could depict sportswomen with gusto and respect, a culture of machismo continued to obstruct women's entry in both print and broadcast media.

TAIWAN—HOME OF PO-CHUN LIU

The Kuomintang (KMT) Chinese Nationalist Party, in power since the end of Japanese rule (1895-1945), began to loosen the reins on military command in the 1970s, gradually incorporating more of the indigenous Taiwanese population. Greater democratization and economic growth helped pave the way for parliamentary reform, and, in 1987, Taiwan saw the end of martial law in favor of a multi-party democratic system.

Cultural attitudes toward women were in flux during Po-Chun's childhood as greater prosperity was accompanied by the increased championing of women's rights, ushered in by the democratic government. The patriarchal system that had long dominated Taiwanese families, rooted in a Confucian culture, was challenged in the mid-twentieth century when a fixed number of seats in parliament were reserved for women. This set Taiwan apart from many other Asian countries in terms of women's participation in government, but still didn't mean that women were considered equal members of society.

Sports, too, had long been considered just for men. Physical activity for women, on the other hand, was welcomed as long as it connected to society's ideals of femininity and beauty. Though 1968 legislation sought to provide girls equal access to education and other opportunities, few arenas outside of the school setting were considered acceptable for women to participate in sports.

First introduced under Japanese occupation in 1897, baseball was originally played by bankers and bureaucrats. By the 1920s, baseball was embraced by all parts of society, despite its ties to the colonial occupier. Although government authorities attempted to wipe the slate clean in 1945, following Japanese rule, baseball remained integral to the Taiwanese identity. Taiwan's international baseball successes in the 1960s and 1970s only increased the sport's standing, and would later serve to invigorate nationalism and patriotism.

BANGLADESH—HOME OF ASHREEN MRIDHA

Bangladesh won independence in 1971 following a bloody war with Pakistan, but a series of military coups starting in 1975 led to a period of political instability. Two decades after becoming a sovereign nation, Bangladesh transitioned to a democratically elected government.

Although Bangladesh is territorially a little smaller than Iowa, it is one of the world's most populous countries. Women playing sports in public were not looked upon favorably by society. As a result, female Bangladeshi athletes were largely absent from the sports landscape, unless it was within the confines of a women's only setting, such as school sports.

Yet, the winds of change that ushered in the new government in the early 1990s also brought the push for greater gender equality. Some strides were made, thanks to the promotion of women's education and health, but progress was slow, and this translated into the sports arena.

The indigenous game of kabaddi, a contact team sport, was chosen as Bangladesh's national game in 1972. However, cricket, a sport first introduced and championed under British colonial rule, was, and remains, king of all sports. Soccer and field hockey were also popular, but all of these team sports were played by men. So, too, were many of the individual sports in which Bangladesh excelled, such as swimming, boxing, and shooting.

KENYA—HOME OF CYNTHIA COREDO

In 1987, Kenya's one-party democratic government, in power since the late 1960s, began to be challenged for human rights abuses and its harsh treatment of political opponents. The struggle for greater democracy crescendoed in December 1991, when a constitutional repeal allowed for greater democratic participation among Kenya's citizens.

Kenyan women were longtime advocates for political change, despite the gender biases ingrained in a deeply patriarchal society. Female organizations, networks, and communities built upon trade and kinship were influential in building opposition to colonial rule, and Kenya won its independence from Great Britain in 1963. The global feminist movement of the 1970s reached Kenya, but changing cultural attitudes were slow to take hold. It was not until the early 1990s that a major shift occurred, due to the formalized roles of women in public life as part of the new government's National Women's Convention in February of 1992.

In sports, Kenyans have always shared a deep pride in their country's athletic excellence at the national and international levels—with its runners winning much acclaim—but actual participation in sport has been geared mostly toward men. The Tokyo Olympics in 1964 saw Kenya participate for the first time as an independent country, though still part of the Commonwealth, its team consisting of 37 men. Kenya's national teams for the 1968 and 1972 Olympics saw little improvement, with only five women participating in total.

Into the 1980s and 1990s, many sports played during the colonial era retained their association with masculinity. Soccer, rugby, field hockey, and boxing, which were accessible to indigenous Kenyans under British rule, were closely associated with violence, and thus not perceived as acceptable for women. While some women had become world-class runners, fewer than ten percent of the athletes on the 1988 Kenyan Olympic Team and the 1990 Commonwealth Games Team were women.

The post-1991 democratization process that led to a resurgence of women in political life also played out in the sports landscape. The Kenyan women's national volleyball team were the undisputed African champions throughout the 1990s, and other disciplines gained popularity as more women and girls overcame obstacles to participate and to pursue training and competition at the highest levels.

BRAZIL—HOME OF ALINE SILVA

Brazil underwent numerous political, sociocultural, and economic changes after 1974 as it transitioned from a dictatorship to a democracy. Brazilians' campaign for economic and social stability put heavy pressure on the military government, in power since 1964, to concede to changes, resulting in the ratification of a constitution in 1988.

This democratic evolution coincided with the rise of the feminist movement. Under the dictatorship, women were cast in stereotypical domestic and feminine roles that centered on the home. After 1970, the push for greater emphasis on human dignity and human rights naturally translated into advocacy for gender equality, and all of these values were enshrined in the new constitution.

In the meantime, sport was seeing a sort of democratization of its own as consumption grew and participation swelled.

The first nationwide sports television broadcasts occurred during the 1970 FIFA World Cup in Mexico, which Brazil won for the third time, solidifying the country as a soccer giant. Brazilian society deemed soccer to be in direct opposition to then-held ideals of femininity, and far too violent and masculine for women and girls to play.

It wasn't just cultural perceptions that wrested women away from engaging in certain sports, it was the law. National legislation enacted in 1941, Decree Law 3199, prohibited women from engaging in sports whose violence might endanger their physical health.

In 1981, the decree was overturned, freeing women and girls to engage in the full spectrum of sporting endeavors, including judo and wrestling. This coincided with more official governance of wrestling in Brazil with the establishment of the Brazilian Wrestling Confederation in 1979 and the inclusion of women's wrestling in international competitions. The first female Brazilian wrestlers competed in a world championship in 1987, though it took nearly two more decades for women's wrestling to be officially recognized as an Olympic sport.

Even though women were allowed to participate in wrestling, they still faced a number of challenges. Wrestling combines strength and certain degrees of aggression, which is why for more than a century it has been viewed in many cultures as a champion of masculinity. Female wrestlers have thus had to prove society wrong, fighting just to get a place on the mat.

VIETNAM—HOME OF NGA LE

Vietnam went through multiple occupations and a bloody war before winning its independence from France in 1954. The following year, it descended into violence again as U.S. forces sought to prevent Ho Chi Minh's communist Viet Cong from gaining traction in the region. Unification of North and South following the Vietnam War brought some healing, but the conflict's aftermath led to hard times for many. Vietnam sank into economic stagnation and international isolation. Most Vietnamese found that opportunities dried up, hopes were dashed, and many had to fight just to survive.

In the mid-1980s, Vietnam was still struggling to put the horrors of a terrible war behind it, but the future was beginning to look a little brighter. Policies of economic liberalization (Doi Moi or "renovation") began to translate into improved livelihoods and greater economic stability for millions of Vietnamese. Society, too, was changing, including long-held notions of what women could and could not do.

On one hand, women's equality had been written into the first constitution of the Democratic Republic of Vietnam (North Vietnam) in 1946, and women were acknowledged as key players in Vietnam's fight for independence. On the other hand, many initiatives to promote the family and improve maternal health and childcare did little to advance equality of the sexes in public life; women were still not gaining entry to the highest levels of government and business or receiving equal pay.

Moreover, any gains originally made under the earlier decades of communist rule were turned back by the "new" feminine ideal of the post-unification period. Based on Confucian values that promoted patriarchy, a renewed emphasis on the family unit meant that women's work and public value were unequal to men, even while they continued to play major labor roles in the Vietnamese economy.

This also impacted women's access and acceptance within the sports world. Soccer is the most popular sport, one that traces its roots back to 1905 when it was introduced under French colonial rule. It was always thought of as one for boys and men, too violent and physical for women. Even in the post-unification period, when the government tried to break with the country's colonial past, soccer remained the dominant sport. Since the late 1980s, the men's national team has done well in international competition, reinforcing the sport's primacy. Shooting, kung fu, and the indigenous sport of da cau are also popularly practiced, and Vietnamese men have experienced success in these disciplines, too.

KUWAIT—HOME OF RABA'A AL HAJERI

This small, strategically located Persian Gulf country, wedged between Saudi Arabia and Iraq, was one of the more prosperous Gulf states, thanks to commercial oil exports. In many ways, it was a society that seemed to be moving backward, with 1950s-era Kuwaiti women enjoying greater liberty and opportunities than their 1990s counterparts.

During the mid-twentieth century, women from the upper classes were routinely educated abroad, often in Egypt, and they brought home the cultural ideas and attitudes to which they had been exposed. By the mid-1950s, the country's first feminist demonstrations made waves in urban Kuwait as scores of women marched, removed their abayas (robe-like dresses), and set fire to them in public protest. Though the new constitutional monarchy pledged equal access to education for women, this was not always adhered to in practice. Moreover, while women in urban areas benefited from higher education, greater wealth, and increased access to the West's changing cultural views toward women, their rural sisters often lagged far behind. Thus, the relatively liberal urban attitudes in Kuwait suffered a disconnect from women's realities in more remote, rural regions.

Cultural transformation was slow, and this included the sports sphere. Traditional sports like camel riding, pearl diving, hunting, shooting, swimming, and diving were widely practiced, but after British colonial administrators introduced soccer in the 1930s, it rapidly became the country's most popular sport. In 1961, Kuwait became independent when it cut ties with the British Empire and formalized sports structures and governance.

Yet, these endeavors were the domain of boys and men. It was not considered appropriate for women to be seen exercising in public in traditional Kuwaiti society. The exception was the practice of sports by girls in "women's only" settings during the decades immediately following independence, which flowered in the 1970s and early 1980s. This coincided with the growth of the global feminist movement and the gradual acceptance of women's physical abilities and independence in Western society.

In February of 1991, a United Nations coalition led by U.S. forces liberated Kuwait and reinstalled the country's constitutional monarchy. Even as society recovered following the liberation, and women entered public life in greater numbers, hardline Islamic ideas continued to stall the advancement towards gender equality. Kuwaiti women watched the progress of female liberation across the Western world, while feeling the stagnation at home.

JORDAN—HOME OF NOOR DAJANI

Officially known as the Hashemite Kingdom of Jordan since its 1921 founding, this Arab country on the East Bank of the Jordan River sits at the crossroads of Asia, Africa, and Europe. While politically stable, the modern-Jordan of the 1980s was at the crux of a mounting economic crisis. Unlike some of its neighboring countries rich in oil and gas, Jordan lacked natural resources.

The state invested heavily in education to ensure that human capital would grow the economy, dispatching Jordanians to work abroad and send home remittances. In turn, well-educated Jordanians began to challenge some of the Muslim-majority nation's long-held cultural gender norms, in which a woman's place had traditionally been in the private realm of the home or in limited public areas such as school or the marketplace.

Change doesn't always happen quickly, and it was still not considered appropriate for girls to play sports in mixed company, as it went against the religious beliefs of many Jordanian families. Further, Jordan's most popular sport by far was, and remains to be, soccer, though it was considered too masculine and too violent for women. Nevertheless, basketball, volleyball, and handball were popular sports that girls were allowed to play within a women only environment, though clubs of this kind were still rare in the Middle East until more recently.

Jordan

ABOUT THE CREATORS

Written by Dr. Sarah Hillyer

Social Change is a Team Sport.

If you know the CSPS already, you know how strongly we feel about the power of teamwork.

If you don't know us yet, hopefully by the time you finish reading *Strong Women. Better World: Title IX's Global Effect*, you'll understand just how passionately we feel about the fact that we are stronger together and, therefore, greater than the sum of our individual parts.

This deeply ingrained belief, rooted in our respective sports experiences, is exactly why we approached this project with a team mindset. The CSPS is a team in pursuit of excellence and winning on behalf of our entire community—all women and girls, no matter where they were born or where they call home. We wanted this project, which expands beyond these pages, to highlight the sisters of the GSMP while also being owned and created by them.

With our philosophical approach top of mind, it is my privilege to introduce you to the worldwide team behind Strong Women. Better World: Title IX's Global Effect.

THE CHIEF DREAM ACHIEVERS:

Ilina Arsova

(Macedonia, GSMP class of 2012): Artist, Illustrator, Writer

Abeer Essawy

(Egypt, GSMP class of 2019): Artist, Digital Illustrator

Carole Ponchon

(France, GSMP class of 2017): Writer, Podcast Host

Carmen "Pina" Pozo

(Bolivia, GSMP class of 2017): Lead Writer

THE DREAM ACHIEVERS:

Hanna Fauzi

(Indonesia, GSMP class of 2015): Writer

Megha Vora

(India, GSMP class of 2017): Writer

Nga Le

(Vietnam, GSMP class of) 2015: Writer

Rabia Qadir

(Pakistan, GSMP class of 2016): Writer

Sangeetha Manoharan

(India, GSMP class of 2017): Writer

Noor Dajani

(Jordan, GSMP class of 2019) Writer

Chisom Mbonu-Ezeoke

(Nigeria, GSMP class of 2017): Podcast Host

THE RESIDENT DREAM ACHIEVERS AND GENDER EQUITY ADVOCATES, AKA THE SUPPORTING CAST:

Dr. Stacey Reece

(Tennessee): Writer, Editor, Curriculum Expert

Dr. Lindsay Krasnoff

(Vermont): Writer, Historian, Sports Diplomacy Expert

Dr. Janine Al-Aseer

(Tennessee): Writer, Editor, Curriculum Expert

Dr. Carolyn Spellings

(Tennessee): Evaluation & Impact Expert

Carly Stucky

(New York): Researcher, Writer, Editor

Carly is one of the most valued magicians behind the scenes. She's thoughtful. She's committed. She's humble. She's skilled. She's "all in" to make sure that every woman in this book, and in our work more broadly, feels empowered, honored, and respected. I've never met anyone more invested in the work than Carly. I am so grateful that she joined our team and I never want to work without her—no matter how we change the world—I want her on my team, always!

Morgan Irish-George

(Kentucky): Book Designer

Morgan is quiet, thoughtful, and carries the weight of excellence in the design of this book on her shoulders. She wants it to be perfect and is afraid to read it after it's out into the world. Why? Because she cares. She cares about excellence. She cares about impact, and she loves the people we impact. I cannot be more grateful for Morgan's commitment to empowering women through sport, education, and media. I am so grateful for the opportunity to work beside her everyday!

Lacey Toves

(Arizona): Organizer, Communicator, Writer, Editor

Lacey is the glue that held all of us together to bring this project from ideation to publication and the one who should teach a masterclass on organizing and effectively communicating thousands of real-time moving parts. Additionally, she's an English major and a genius editor. She pays attention to detail and cares about excellence from the bottom of her heart. Without Lacey, this project doesn't happen, and, more importantly, it doesn't happen with the excellence we're able to deliver. So proud. Never want to be without you in this work to change the world.

With the team-assigned title of Dream Blurter, I couldn't be prouder of this group. They took my vision for a multi-modal project and devised a game plan based on the diverse strengths of each person involved. Further, they used the power of the pen as a means to celebrate the modern-day gender equity and sports pioneers highlighted in this book.

ACKNOWLEDGMENTS

Written by Dr. Sarah Hillyer

We have many people to thank for helping us bring the *Strong Women. Better World: Title IX's Global Effect* storytelling and research project to life. Here's our roster of sporty, and much appreciated, change-makers:

In the beginning…

A huge thank you to Beth Fine, former Program Officer at the U.S. Department of State Sports Diplomacy Division (formerly SportsUnited). Without your vision, belief, and determination, the GSMP would not exist, and without the GSMP, this book would not exist.

Loads of gratitude to Dr. Bob Rider, former Dean of the University of Tennessee College of Education, Health & Human Sciences. Without your profound trust and willingness to support my vision for a center dedicated to using the power of sport and education to create a more equitable, inclusive, and peaceful world, we would not be celebrating ten years of the CSPS. Without you, this book doesn't happen, and without this book readers miss the opportunity to learn about the global effect of Title IX for women around the world fighting for their own gender equity moments. Dr. Dixie Thompson, Dr. Joy DeSensi and Dr. Dulcie Peccolo – my deep appreciation for your love and support every step of the way (Dr. D and Dr. Peccolo, I miss you so much and wish you were here to

celebrate this moment with us!). You were the mentors I always dreamed of having, and I will forever be grateful for each of you.

Last but not least, Dr. Ashleigh Huffman. Dr. Ash, your contributions to help shape what the GSMP has become are undeniable. I will forever be grateful for the beautiful memories we made over the years and across continents and the collective impact we've made, all while realizing the higher calling in our lives to serve people for purposes beyond the here and now. Thank you for your energy, intellect, and investment in the work to advance women's rights. Godspeed to you—keep doing amazing things, like you do. I'm so proud.

Readers, Reviewers & Really Awesome Allies

We are incredibly grateful for UT Press, specifically for Thomas Wells and Kelly Gray. Your commitment to promoting diversity, equity, and inclusion is unparalleled. You understood our mission from the very beginning and offered your expertise and support in ways that surpassed all expectations. Honestly, we couldn't be luckier to have you as our teammates in this project.

Thank you to the Under Armour dream-team of reviewers and readers who volunteered their precious time to help us proofread and perfect the final product, line by line. Lynn Quayle, thank you for your leadership and for all of the laughter along the way. You and your team—Jennifer Drapisch, Mahmood Abdul, Hayley Gillmore, Xena Kyryk, and Jamie Suthard—are making a difference in the world, and we couldn't be more grateful. Here's to many more world-changing projects together. Watch out world!

Thanks to our new Sports Diplomacy Program Officer, Debbie Drucker, for your sharp editing skills and deep institutional, cultural, and historical insights. Even though we just started working together, we already love your heart—you are humble, thoughtful, kind and wise. Thank you and welcome to the team!

Superhero Supporters

A huge and heartfelt thanks, with lots of high-fives, to: John Lisko, Dr. Nancy Major, Ken Romanzi, Val Ackerman, Susan Cohig, Carol Stiff, Dr. Jill Brooks, Joan Coraggio, Romina Bongiovanni, Leah LaPlaca, Marina Escobar, Lindsay Amstutz, Jennifer Pransky, John Register, Susan Dakak, Beth Curry, Beth McClinton, Scott Carmichael, Allison Jones, Tina Acosta, Mike Mushett, Karen Morrison, Julie Eddleman, Diane Cummins, Lynn Quayle, Dr. Allison Barber, Jules Morris, Joan Cronan, and Karen and Ralph Weekly. And my parents, Michael and Jackie; and nephew Jonah.

Deep Bench

All championship teams have depth, and our team of sporty change-makers is no exception. A special thanks to:

Trina Bolton, former Program Officer at the U.S. Department of State Sports Diplomacy Division and instrumental player in the growth of the GSMP. Without you, Trina, the GSMP's global impact would not be fully realized. You dedicated years to the program and were a tireless advocate for our work to share the lessons of Title IX beyond our own borders. You lived your passion, you leveraged your platform, and you fulfilled your purpose as a public servant to advance the rights of women around the world.

The dream-team at the Women's Basketball Hall of Fame: Dana Hart, Danielle Haas, and Josh Sullivan. Thank you for being our behind-the-scenes fiscal partners and making the organized chaos happen with efficiency and absolute integrity.

The high-powered team at espnW: Jane Bullock, Rachel Epstein, and Laura Gentile. Thank you for lending the strength of ESPN's brand to the GSMP and for identifying the best mentors in the world. Jane, a special thanks to you for being such a great partner in the day-to-day work. Your genuine care and concern for our GSMP sisters is refreshing and much appreciated—you never lose sight of the humanity of the task at hand—and for this, I appreciate you more than you'll ever know!

The Sports Diplomacy Team at the State Department (Matt M., Cindy, May, Ray, Ryan, Matt F., Jay, and Robert) and the respective Cultural Affairs Teams at more than 90 U.S. Embassies around the world. You are the unsung heroes of this work—public servants who quietly and humbly advance peace through your commitment to the local communities and countries you serve.

Every student and young professional who has ever been a member of the CSPS Team. Though there are too many to name, you know who you are, and we couldn't be more grateful for your contributions. Without you, we wouldn't be able to celebrate more than 450,000 lives impacted through the CSPS over the past ten years. Keep dancing, laughing, and using your passion, platform, and purpose to create a better world!

Every person who has ever supported us at UT. The late Pat Summitt, Chancellor Dondie Plowman, President Randy Boyd, Provost John Zomchick, Dr. Sherry Bell, Dr. David Bassett, Dr. Ellen McIntyre, Dr. Kristina Gordon, Dr. Hollie Raynor, Dr. Gretchen Neisler, Jamie McGowen, Courtney Holbert, and Dawn Hawkersmith; and to the selfless "Dean's Suite" staff quietly making it all happen behind the scenes: Emily Mason, Nancy Thomas, Diane Booker, and Debbie Archdale.

Program Partners

Carmen Sturniolo, founder of Ambitious Athletics and the strongest (literally and figuratively) male ally I've ever met. Thank you for believing in every GSMP sister and helping each of them dig deep, fight through the pain, and prove to themselves that they are capable of doing much more than they ever imagined.

Susan Dunlap, the amazing team at the YMCA Anthony Bowen in DC (Angie Reese-Hawkins and Allison Jones), John White and the brilliant adaptive sports teachers at Prince George County Schools, and Eli Wolff.

Social change is a team sport and we couldn't imagine doing this work without each of you. The same goes for the countless additional people who have influenced our lives and who weren't mentioned here. Thanks to all—let's keep changing the world together through the power of sport and education!